# WORK YOUR MAGIC

# Create a **Better** **Business Community** That Works for **Everyone**

## SHARON DARMODY

SHE WRITES PRESS

Published 2023
Printed in the United States of America
Print ISBN: 978-1-64742-533-3
E-ISBN: 978-1-64742-534-0
Library of Congress Control Number: 2023910548

For information, address:
She Writes Press
1569 Solano Ave #546
Berkeley, CA 94707

Interior Design by Tabitha Lahr

She Writes Press is a division of SparkPoint Studio, LLC.

"Autobiography in Five Chapters"
From THERE'S A HOLE IN MY SIDEWALK: THE ROMANCE OF SELF-DISCOVERY by Portia Nelson. Copyright © 1993 by Portia Nelson. Reprinted with the permission of Beyond Words/Atria Books, a division of Simon & Schuster, Inc. All rights reserved.

To all those people who go to work every day and try their best!

# CONTENTS

# INTRODUCTION

# A NEW WORK ORDER

*There comes a point where we need to stop just pulling people out of the river. We need to go upstream and find out why they're falling in.*[1]
**—DESMOND TUTU**

In March 2020, working life as we knew it ground to a shuddering halt. In an attempt to control the spread of the novel coronavirus that sent shockwaves around the world, businesses across all industries were forced to shut up shop, with hundreds of millions of employees globally being laid off, furloughed, or—for the lucky ones—instructed to carry out their roles from home. As disruptive as this was, for many white-collar workers, this created a sudden and unprecedented opportunity to radically rethink every aspect of their working lives in real time. From flexible office hours to a focus on worker well-being, all was now up for grabs. But despite having worked with teams and individuals on tackling these exact issues for decades, now that the way ahead had been cleared, very few people seemed ready or willing to pave a new path.

One client even shared with me that while he, like everybody else in his department, was working from home, he had stuck to his "commute"—traveling into the office and back home every morning to set himself up for the working day. In other instances, I found myself helping others set boundaries around their work time, so the day didn't blur into a haze of homeschooling and late-night emails. But the fact that this particular individual would go to such lengths to maintain his "normal" routine made me realize how wedded the majority of us still were to the idea that the working day must look a certain way. If a global pandemic wasn't enough to shake up the status quo and get us curious about new ways in which to live and work, what would be?

Even outside of work, COVID provided most of us with an opportunity for a reset, as if the pause button had been hit on life as we knew it. Even for those who were able to work consistently during lockdown, many of the pressures and obligations of the external world fell away. In this, we were able to reassess our priorities and to notice where we had been frittering our time and energy away. We noticed what truly was essential to our lives and saw where we had just been going through the motions.

More than anything, many people I was working with at the time recognized that they had taken their work connections for granted. Meanwhile, getting a window into people's home lives over Zoom reminded us that our colleagues were human beings just like us—with pets, kids, potted plants, and, maybe, funny hats. We remembered that work was as much about community as it was about commerce and that it was a place where we could find meaning, fun, and even joy. By the time we got to press "play" again, most of us had recognized that we were ready for some changes to our working lives—changes that would mean less mindless clocking in of hours and more of the human interactions and ingenuity that are what really make work *work*. But with one foot still stuck in the old way of doing things and so many unknowns ahead of us, where, exactly, were we supposed to go? What we needed was a clear road map forward and a "new work order."

My vision for this? In a post-COVID world, I believe it is time to reimagine the workplace so that each individual is an active participant in shaping the culture and so the choices made on behalf of the company take our needs and our *humanity* into account. Far from making us less productive, this is about bringing our whole selves to the office (virtual or not) and not just singing along to somebody else's playbook. I've seen firsthand that for a company's culture to work, it must work for every last individual on the team. If anything, the pandemic of 2020 was a wake-up call: if our workplace doesn't speak to who we are and what's important to us as human beings first and foremost, then work just isn't working.

For all the trauma, stress, and uncertainty ushered in by the pandemic, the overarching theme of this enforced timeout was that we got to see exactly what wasn't working about the way we had been working. By shining a spotlight on the workplace habits and routines we had adopted but not necessarily chosen, we could see that while some of these old ways of working helped keep things running smoothly, others had pushed us toward exhaustion and burnout. The year 2020 allowed us all to step away from what we were used to, to breathe for a moment, and to view the workplace and our relationship with work with beginner's eyes. What if, instead of racing to resume business as usual, we took these insights and used them to forge a whole new way of working? From where I'm sitting, this is a necessary change that has been a long time coming.

Since I began my business as an organizational consultant and mediator in 2004, my role has been to work with both individuals and teams to support people in becoming more engaged and really thriving at work. Over the past eighteen years, I have seen firsthand the fallout from focusing on profit and progress at the cost of people's needs and well-being. In the same way climate change has wreaked havoc on the natural world, many of us knew that the way we were operating our businesses, our working lives, was not sustainable. Often by the time I was called in, people were already experiencing the symptoms of burnout: anxiety, depression, addiction, or a myriad of other health problems. These "people" problems lead to business problems—which may seem obvious but which most business systems fail to recognize. When our team members are thriving, business thrives—and the reverse is also true. When teams are made up of people who are uninspired and depleted, there is no focus, no cohesion, no connectedness, and, dare I say it, no fun.

The majority of workplaces have not been set up to support a dynamic where people and businesses are *both* able to prosper in the long term. From my vantage point, I could see that in many cases, this meant both were beginning to drown. Sometimes, this looked like people literally going under, becoming unwell, and needing time away from work to recover. But even in corporate environments where systems appeared to be working on the surface, I often found people and projects alike gasping for air. I encountered teams where innovation and creativity had been replaced by default systems and ways of doing things that left no space for people to feel like active participants in their own working lives. Leaving people feeling ignored, insecure, and like there was no space for "them" at work, this often resulted in conflict, backstabbing, lack of productivity, and passive-aggressive behavior.

At its most effective, my work is largely focused on helping organizations to stop just "pulling people out of the river" and to engage in the sort of problem-solving that stops people from falling in in the first place. And over my years of working with individuals, teams, and organizations, I began to realize that what was often missing from corporate life was the *magic* touch. Or rather, MAGIC, which is my acronym for what I believe are the core drivers of people being engaged and thriving at work: Meaning, Authenticity, Ground Rules, "I," and Curiosity.

Coming at it through the lens of occupational therapy, I consistently found that it was working with these specific elements that helped to get people, their teams, and their businesses back on track. Why? In short, I could see that MAGIC was the missing foundational piece in an entirely new approach to integrating people's humanity with the expectations and demands of corporate life. And 2020 fast-tracked this shift, forcing us to think on our feet as we were asked to completely reimagine the relationships between our work lives and our home lives, between the hats we wear at work and the human beings we are on the inside. So where do we go from here?

I am able to achieve the best outcomes when I get to work with people before burnout has set in or when teams are able to explore the benefits of MAGIC before they hit rock bottom. But as a workplace mediator, I am often called in when things have already blown up. Nine times out ten, when I speak with the people involved, they know where they have gone wrong and that they should not have acted the way they did, said what they said, or sent quite so blunt an email. But they felt so "out of control," they tell me, that they did it anyway, without considering the long-term consequences of how the situation might play out. When we are able to sit quietly together, how they should have responded becomes crystal clear. But this is when the truth also begins to emerge, and I hear the stories of people not sleeping, of there being tension at home, of people drinking too much, and of the physical and mental health problems that all too often go hand in hand with problems at work.

I remember one client describing her Monday morning to me. Facing down another working week, she braced herself, telling herself: "You can do it—you can get through this." As she described this she literally clenched her fists, her body language speaking volumes about her mental state. Try clenching your fist, right now, and just holding tight for a minute or so. It's not comfortable, and it's certainly not enjoyable. Yet I've met so many people who approach their working lives this way, bracing themselves against life, fists balled up and clinging on tight. Is it any wonder that things blow up when the going gets tough?

By the time we get to this place, one or more of the elements of MAGIC is often missing. This acronym essentially describes the simple human systems that make work *work*, which have often been usurped by dogged focus on productivity and the bottom line. So often when I get called in, whether to work with an individual person or a team, I hear of things just not having "been right" for quite some time. But there had been no time for pause, no review of the wider company culture, and no consideration that it might be time to take stock, to reflect, and to course correct.

What I discovered was that in providing a framework for exactly how to do this, it was often quite clear what needed to change and what steps needed to be taken to get there. Even better, it usually didn't mean breaking everything apart and starting all over again. More often than not, quite subtle changes could make an enormous difference. But now, with old ways of working having been dismantled literally overnight, we have the opportunity to rebuild our businesses with MAGIC woven into the foundations from the ground up—leading to healthier and more productive ways of working for us all.

The World Health Organization (WHO) describes the relationship between work, health, and productivity as a virtuous cycle, where "improved conditions at work will lead to a healthier work force, which will lead to improved productivity, and hence the opportunity to create a still healthier, more productive workplace."[2] Who knew it would take a global health pandemic to bring home the truth of this statement? When considering whether our workplace supports this virtuous cycle, we might first look to the policies, procedures, and programs that are in place to support people while they're at work. However, the kind of lasting, sustainable change that will enable businesses to truly thrive far into the future will require evolution at DNA level. Rather than continue to make tweaks to existing systems, we now have an unprecedented opportunity to rebuild and reboot our working lives.

Chances are, your business experienced uncertainty like never before in 2020. In many instances, systems we had relied on, particularly when it came to communication, team structures, and decision-making, needed to be rethought. And if anything, what we realized during this time was that we need ways of working that truly support us as individuals and that in turn we can depend on to support us in every aspect of our lives. Now, as we move forward and recover together, I believe we can achieve this by building the elements of MAGIC into our workplaces from the ground up.

This means so much more than simply implementing new policies and procedures. At the very least it will be a case of understanding where we're at, how we got here, and being honest about the problems we face. It will mean seeking to answer big questions about who we are and what we believe in, as individuals and as organizations, as well as tending to the small details of how we treat ourselves and one another day-to-day. In some cases, it will require us to reimagine and remake each and every aspect of our working lives, as we take this opportunity to completely overhaul whatever is no longer working.

So why MAGIC? All magicians know that magic—the kind that leaves people feeling like they've witnessed the impossible—isn't something that "just happens." The ability to wow an audience and pull rabbits out of hats is actually the result of dedicated practice. It also means following a specific formula in an ordered and consistent manner, and whether you are a member of a team or someone who leads a team (or perhaps somewhere in between), you can think of this book as your Harry Potter manual for bringing more MAGIC to your workplace.

Along with an in-depth explanation of each of the tenets of Meaning, Authenticity, Ground Rules, "I," and Curiosity, I will be providing real-life examples of how I have used them to help reinvigorate teams, boost productivity, and help people feel happier at work overall. I will show you ways to support yourself, your team, and even the whole organization as you implement these elements, and, in the chapters dedicated to these practices, you will also find easy-to-follow exercises and applications for introducing them day by day.

As we continue to reorganize the ways we work and step into this new phase of corporate life, you may even find you have intuitively been using some of these tools already—and, in doing so, uncovering some of the pieces that have been missing in your workplace up until now. So often when I work with people, they know exactly what they could and should be doing; what's needed is for them to pause, step off the hamster wheel of the default mode of doing things, and once again become active participants in choosing how they want to work and determining the role they want work to play in their lives. And now we have the opportunity to do exactly that.

After all, if anything, the events of 2020 have left us all feeling a little more human. As work and home life have been blurred, we've remembered that the person we are in the office is the very same person who has a life back home. We have seen firsthand that our performance and happiness at work is directly linked to the quality of our home life, and vice versa, and that *everything* works better when we feel fully supported in all of our needs. In our isolation, we've also realized the importance of genuine human connection—the kind where we feel understood and accepted for who we truly are. This, indeed, is magic. And in these realizations, there is no more avoiding that the old ways of doing things just won't cut it.

We were ready for change long before the pandemic changed everything, forever. We were ready for work to work *better*. May this book be your guide to implementing the changes that will make the impossible a reality for you and your workplace, be it over the long term or in your day-to-day. And as we find ways to recover from the COVID-19 pandemic together, may the insights in these pages convince you to expect some MAGIC and miracles along the way.

## CHAPTER 1

# THE WAY WE'VE BEEN WORKING
# HASN'T BEEN WORKING

*A 2018 Gallup study revealed 85 percent of employees function below their potential and don't feel engaged at work.[1]*

**—WILLIAM CRAIG, *FORBES* MAGAZINE**

Let's sit with this Gallup statistic for a moment. *This means almost nine out of ten people in your workplace are essentially just going through the motions.* Is this the best we can do, for ourselves or our workplaces? I don't think so; I have more faith in us and our ability to thrive professionally and personally at work. Clearly, there is room for improvement, but if we really are going to stop people from "falling in the river," we need to understand why they're burning out and falling in in the first place. When it comes to how we work, how have we lost our way?

Most of the people I work with would readily admit that life just isn't working for them. They often feel like bystanders in their own lives, watching from the sidelines and unable to keep up. Of course, most of the time you would never know this from the outside. To a casual observer, they are often leading what many would think of as sought-after lives, with high-profile positions, enviable homes, regular holidays, and family lives overflowing with Instagrammable activities. But behind the scenes, they are experiencing a slow, internal crumbling. They have reached a point where they know something has to give and that it's only a matter of time before things fall apart and they get found out for not having it all together after all. They know something needs to change, but they don't know what that is or where to start.

Viktor Frankl said, "Between stimulus and response there is space. In that space is our power to choose our response. In our response lies our growth and our freedom."[2] And I don't think anyone I either work with or know through my social circle feels that there is much "space" in their life. People tell me that they are constantly in catch-up mode and that this does not feel good. I hear again and again that after one fire has been put out and the adrenaline washes away, they feel exhausted and a little empty, but that before they know it the next fire is starting to burn, and they are off again. This feeling of constantly playing catch-up does not provide the space for the sort of decision-making that makes a difference in our lives—whether this applies to individuals or teams and businesses.

I often ask my clients to picture a seesaw and then see themselves standing in the middle. As kids, this can be a lot of fun, as we wobble and topple off in fits of giggles. But by the time we're adults, juggling work with home and family life, while trying to carve out time for our passions on the side, trying to keep the seesaw balanced so we don't come crashing down takes a lot of energy. It's exhausting. I go on to explain that in our work together, we will be building some blocks to put under each end of the seesaw, and that with these in place, everything will feel more stable. They will be able to relax a little, lower their shoulders, and take a big, deep breath. Life will still be happening, but keeping everything up in the air just won't be so exhausting. Sounds appealing, doesn't it? Of course, some people discover they are actually on the wrong seesaw altogether, have perhaps even gotten lost in the wrong playground, and that they need to make some bigger changes. However, from my experience I've learned that most people are able to find profound relief and a greater sense of stability with some small modifications to the ways they have been working.

This can all be achieved through working with the principles of MAGIC. But before we get into the details of how to apply each of the pillars of Meaning, Authenticity, Ground Rules, "I," and Curiosity, let's return to how we got ourselves into a situation where everything feels so shaky in the first place. Even before the pandemic of 2020, there were a number of threats looming over the workplace that were preventing us from feeling supported at work and, in turn, from living fully engaging and satisfying lives. It would be a mistake to blame all of our problems on the ruptures to the way we work caused by the bug. But if we are to avoid simply falling back into the same old patterns post-COVID, we must be fully cognizant of the factors that have destabilized our working lives. Only when we are able to observe and to name what's been going on will we be able to manage and disrupt the workplace behaviors that keep finding people falling through the cracks. This will leave us in a better position to make the kind of decisions that will support us to thrive as we rebuild our workplaces and our lives. So let's take a closer look at why the way we've been working hasn't been working.

In my experience, there are three specific areas that have taken us down the wrong track. While these individual influences may not have the earth-shattering impact of the pandemic, they have certainly become *epidemics*, and as such they have taken their toll on the overall well-being and productivity of teams and the individual employees that are the life-force of the workplace. They are:

- the mental health epidemic
- the loneliness epidemic
- the tech epidemic

Let's take a closer look at how the emergence of these three factors clearly demonstrates how we have lost our way.

## THE MENTAL HEALTH EPIDEMIC

The World Health Organization has indicated that depression and unipolar depressive disorders will move into first place as the leading cause of the global burden of disease by 2030. Given that burnout was also named an official "syndrome" by the WHO in 2019—with symptoms that include feelings of energy depletion or exhaustion; increased mental distance from one's job, or feelings of negativism or cynicism related to one's job; and reduced professional efficacy—this paints an alarming picture about the state of workers' mental health.

Now consider this: Reams of research now proves without question that there are tremendous health benefits to being actively employed that support not only our mental health but also our physical health. In 2006, Gordon Waddell and Kim Burton were commissioned by the UK's Department for Work and Pensions to conduct an independent review of the scientific evidence into whether work was good for your health and well-being. At the time, there was a growing awareness that (long-term) worklessness is harmful to physical and mental health, and the study hoped to prove that the corollary might also be assumed—that employment is beneficial for health.

Waddell and Burton's research shows that unemployment does indeed have a significant negative impact on both physical and mental health, and it even results in increased mortality rates. People experiencing periods of unemployment were not only more likely to suffer from higher incidences of chronic health conditions, such as cardiovascular disease, respiratory infections, and some cancers; they were also more likely to die by suicide. The study also recognized that in addition to being our means of obtaining economic resources, work also meets our psychosocial needs, is central to our individual identity, and supports our social roles and status. Not only is work good for our physical well-being, but it is also beneficial from a mental health perspective.[3]

But if research shows that work is what keeps us healthy and sane, how is it that so many people feel dissatisfied—if not downright distressed—on the job? Layer in the WHO data on overall mental health, and there is clearly more to this story. When did work stop being a boost to our well-being and the mental health epidemic creep into the workplace?

For many of us, there are times at work where either the demands of the job itself or the people we work with have a detrimental impact on our life. It may feel as if what is happening at work follows us home from the office and, in some cases, literally makes us feel sick. Perhaps it starts with a light uneasiness before bed on a Sunday night, slowly developing up over time to constant feelings of anxiety and overwhelm or symptoms such as nausea or headaches. Then these start to kick in on Sunday morning or lunch time—or whenever it is you start to contemplate returning to work on Monday morning. If you're able to leave work at work, you may not start feeling a pressure in your chest or a knot in your stomach until you walk back into the office.

If this is you, you are not alone. Many of my clients tell me they seek pain relief for headaches as a routine part of their week, while others say they don't eat during the workday because they "have no appetite" or just know the food won't go down. Others think sleep is just for the weekend, or perhaps they often wake in the night, the adrenaline pumping and their mind racing with everything on their to-do list. Many see three or four glasses of wine as the "only thing" that will allow them to wind down after the workday. And while many of these scenarios have become "normal," simply the side effects of the job, it is not supposed to be this way.

What concerns me most is that we've come to see the concept of "work" as something that depletes us and that we almost expect to take a toll on our physical and mental health. Which is a far cry from the research that suggests work has the capacity to support our mental well-being. Particularly alarming is that these coping mechanisms having become expected, meaning people are often suffering in silence. They often don't perceive themselves as having a problem until it's too late and they've experienced some kind of a breakdown. What's more, as long as their productivity remains high, no one knows what it takes for them to get their work done.

A contributing factor has been that work culture has steadily become less about the people, with a singular focus on the output of a business. But ironically, worrying about the deliverables with no recognition of the needs of the people doing the delivering means there is very little chance of a satisfactory or quality outcome. People have also become expendable, the underlying message being that there's always somebody else waiting in the wings if for any reason we can't perform. But at what cost? If we're looking at the bottom line, Employee Benefits News reported in 2017 that turnover can cost employers 33 percent of an employee's annual salary.[4] In the long run, it's much more cost effective to invest in the people you've got. After all, my experience has shown me that the success of any business is the sum of the people putting in the hours behind the scenes. But with an ever-narrowing focus on the bottom line, we've been too distracted by spreadsheets and data to notice employees' eyes slowly dulling, as the spark of connection and creativity that used to be the hallmark of a thriving workplace has been all but extinguished.

Post-COVID, the focus has been on how to safeguard our workplaces against physical infection, with stringent handwashing and social distancing measures. How about if we paid the same attention to looking after our company culture and safeguarding employees' mental health? For many, 2020 proved to be the most challenging year of their lives. Coming out of isolation, people are wondering who they are and where they fit in. If workplaces don't attend to some of these questions in a proactive way, the World Health Organization's prediction for the future in terms of mental health will be a drop in the ocean. As we submit our guidelines for social distancing and the cleaning of surfaces to allow people to return to work safely, knowing everything is being done to protect them from the coronavirus, we also need to put in a plan to support people feeling seen and connected in their workplaces. This is what will allow them to feel safe from a psychological perspective.

This needn't require a wholesale tearing down of everything we have been doing. Time and again in my work, I've seen how simply paying attention to our people and putting practices in place to seal up the gaps and to course correct is often enough. Experience has proven to me that when work becomes a place where we feel valued and seen, and where there is connection with both the people and the broader contribution of the business, both people and projects begin to thrive. Given the current state of play, it would seem that these crucial elements are often what's missing. In fairness, this has not necessarily been by design. It's not as if CEOs and business owners consciously set out to divide workforces, prevent people from feeling like they're making a meaningful contribution, and leave employees feeling anxious and depressed. Rather, more often than not I walk into workplaces where unhealthy systems have become entrenched, the side-effects of which have snow-balled over a period of time. Left unchecked, bad habits have a tendency to creep up on us. And when we're oper-ating so fast there's hardly space to breathe, these habits simply continue unchecked.

For example, under Workplace Health and Safety reg-ulations, every workplace has a responsibility to provide a safe working environment and systems. The definition of "health" in this instance extends to preventing psychological harm.[5] However, I have seen that the way to prevent psy-chological harm at work—and safeguard the mental health of employees—is not tick-a-box resilience training, as often seems like the "obvious" solution (even as it just encourages employees to take on more and more). Rather, it lies in fastidious and conscious work and organizational design. This refers to organizing tasks, systems, and structures so that people have some level of control and autonomy at work; clarifying roles and responsibilities; and improving supervision and workplace relationships.

But these skills are not instinctive, and changing what hasn't been working often demands real focus and plan-ning. Workplaces need a framework to build, or perhaps rebuild, a healthy and safe workplace. MAGIC provides this framework, both for teams and individuals, and can be implemented at any and in fact every stage of a person's life cycle at an organization, right from the time they apply for the job until they leave. But to be truly effective, this approach must become part of an organization's DNA—and not be thought of as a Band-Aid to be applied when something has gone wrong.

When approached this way, there is an opportunity for the workplace not only to operate at optimum productivity but also to become once again a platform that has a positive impact on an individual's and a community's mental health. The question, as we survey our options in a post-pandemic world, is whether workplaces will be willing to pick up this torch and run with it.

Wherever we fall on the spectrum of having been impacted by the pandemic, 2020 left us all feeling a little more vulnerable and a little more human. Even those among us who may have felt invincible discovered that they too are susceptible to the pressure of unprecedented external forces. But this has actually created a window of opportunity for us to thread our humanness back into the workplace and to commit to doing things a little differently for the greater good.

And for those whose primary focus remains fixed on the bottom line, let's look at some more research. According to the WHO, mental health disorders are the leading cause of work disability and are predicted to cost the global economy up to an estimated A $23 trillion by 2030.[6] Which gives further insight into the true cost of the mental health epidemic.

## THE LONELINESS EPIDEMIC

What does loneliness mean in the twenty-first century? Dr. Michelle H. Lim, scientific chair of the Australian Coalition to End Loneliness, identifies it as the next public health epidemic of the twenty-first century.[7] So how is it that being lonely can impact our health so significantly? The research in this area is compelling, and it is also a call to anybody interested in health and well-being in the workplace to sit up and pay attention to the loneliness epidemic.

Let's look more closely at the impact of loneliness.

There is evidence to suggest that loneliness is associated with a 26 percent increase in a person's likelihood of mortality. Research from 2015 by Julianne Holt-Lunstad, Timothy B. Smith, Mark Baker, Tyler Harris, and David Stephenson shows that loneliness increases our risk of experiencing poorer health outcomes from decreased immunity, increased inflammatory response, elevated blood pressure, decreases in cognitive health, and faster progression of Alzheimer's disease. It is no surprise that higher levels of loneliness are also related to more severe mental health symptoms. While loneliness is most commonly examined in terms of depression, anxiety has been found to also play a role, with evidence from large population studies indicating that anxiety increases the odds of feeling lonely.[8]

When we see the broad impact of loneliness on our health, it becomes obvious that it is also a missing piece in the puzzle of why work isn't working. You might think that workplaces, where people typically congregate and experience daily social interaction, would be exempt from loneliness. If anything, most of us have tried to find a little "quiet time" in the office at some point. Furthermore, as a place where we come together, isn't the workplace in a prime position to actually have an impact on this impending threat?

But we must consider the following questions: Are we coming together in a meaningful way? Do we really "see" our colleagues, or are we just going through the motions, too "busy" to recognize that there are human beings working alongside us. As bosses and team leaders, do we set up systems to allow people to be seen by one another at work, for people to get to know one another, and to celebrate the differences people bring to their teams? Or is everyone expected to mold themselves into some sort of company clone, like robots who are solely there to get the job done?

If it's the latter, this usually isn't malicious or even conscious; it simply often feels easier to contain or control the workforce when people's individual personalities are erased. But if people feel they need to shrink or hide themselves to "fit in," then we are actually encouraging loneliness in our workplaces. In addition, when employees are turning themselves inside out to fit in at work, we have also killed innovation. Creativity is all about seeing things differently and being curious about life—including the person at the workstation next to us.

So how does a lack of appreciation for our fellow humans relate to the loneliness epidemic? It can be that we're simply moving too fast to make a connection, or spending too much time looking into a screen versus looking into another person's eyes. Loneliness can also set in when we're too focused on the Instagram world, comparing ourselves to the "picture-perfect" lives of others and failing to recognize that they are in fact walking a similar road—beset with struggles—to us, a road with ups and downs and twists and turns and dead ends where you have to spin around and start again. We think of loneliness as affecting those who live alone, or who perhaps don't have many other people in their lives. But it can equally be applied to somebody who is surrounded by people but who feels separated from them in this cycle of toxic comparison. Loneliness can affect anybody who is lacking deep and meaningful connections—a situation that is all too prevalent in the world we live in today. On the surface, we have never been more well networked, but in reality, it has never been harder to truly connect.

Let's go back to the numbers to see how this could be impacting your workplace.

The 2018 Australian Loneliness Report revealed that one in four Australians reported feeling lonely each week.[9] Of course, this is not just an Australian problem but a global one. Loneliness affects almost half of adult Americans, with MDLinx, a news service for physicians, reporting: "The [loneliness] epidemic in America now affects up to 47% of adults—double the number affected just a few decades ago."[10]

The impact of this? In his book *Lost Connections*, Johann Hari recounts research from John Cacioppo, director of the Center for Cognitive and Social Neuroscience at the University of Chicago, that shows how feeling lonely can cause cortisol levels to soar—as much as the most disturbing or traumatic events a person may experience. Now imagine an office full of people feeling silently *traumatized* by loneliness. If, as Cacioppo's research shows, becoming acutely lonely can be as stressful as experiencing a physical attack, they may be operating in either fight, flight, or freeze mode.[11] We've probably all seen this play out at work; maybe somebody lashes out at another team member, another person is frozen and unable to take the initiative, or another simply avoids getting involved all together. All of these are signs pointing to the loneliness epidemic; in cases like these, it is as if our *instinct for connection* has atrophied.

Now, if somebody had a physical problem that was contributing to difficulties at work, such as being on crutches because of a broken leg, we would make it easier for them to get around, setting up their workstation to make sure they had access to the bathrooms and the kitchen. But because we can't see the underlying causes of a person's psychological issues, it's easier to write these people off, dismissing issues such as the ones outlined above as discipline or performance problems. We know something is not right, but we look the other way, while labeling a person who behaves this way as a "loose cannon" or "not a team player." This is a grave mistake, as these kinds of symptoms are a flashing neon sign telling us that it's time to ask what we could be doing differently in our workplace.

In fact, if organizations truly understood the full implications of the loneliness epidemic—and its potential impact on business outcomes—they would be lining up to do something about it. If those of you with the bottom line more at the front of your mind need any more convincing, it also turns out that lonely people are three times more likely to catch the flu than people with lots of close connections. Considering the potential cost of sick days and company-subsidized flu shots, actively addressing loneliness and promoting connection in your workplace might be a cost-efficient solution to fighting the winter bugs. But again, given that loneliness is on the rise, it would appear that whatever we are doing at work is currently *contributing* to the problem as opposed to helping solve it.

What we need to be doing instead is setting up systems that address the loneliness epidemic from the moment people set foot in the workplace. We need to lean *toward* people, not look away, so that they begin to feel really seen by others in their workplaces. After all, work *is* still one of the few places where people have an opportunity to interact and connect with others on a daily basis. While increasing numbers of people working remotely, or pursuing freelance careers, could be a contributing factor to this increase in loneliness, the International Labour Organization shows that 61 percent of people worldwide are engaged with workplaces where they have the opportunity for connection.[12] Furthermore, at a time when connections to many other community spaces, such as church or even neighborhood groups, have fallen away, the workplace is one of the few remaining places where human interaction could be deemed essential. It seems obvious therefore that this also provides an opportunity to address the loneliness epidemic with our approach to work. And MAGIC also provides the pillars to do just this.

## THE TECH EPIDEMIC

Given the extent to which we all came to rely on technology to stay connected during the COVID-19 pandemic, the subject of the tech epidemic feels like a double-edged sword. However, most of us have been in meetings where people pay more attention to their phones than the subject on the table. Likewise, we've all had the experience of being in the middle of a conversation with somebody and having a notification from their phone immediately take their attention away from us. As helpful as technology can be, whether from a focus perspective or from a human perspective, the cumulative impact of repeatedly choosing our phones over remaining available to what or who is in front of us has resulted in us losing agency over our focus, our energy, and our attention. And when we're no longer in control of this, then are we really in control of our lives?

Your response may be that it's simply our responsibility to stay on top of it. To notice when we've been sucked in too far and to take a time out to course correct. But the tech epidemic is a lot more sinister than that. In the words of Tristan Harris, a former Google product manager who's now working to raise awareness about how our devices are designed to manipulate us, "Your telephone in the 1970s didn't have a thousand engineers on the other side of the telephone who were redesigning it . . . to be more and more persuasive."[13] Our inability to keep our attention off our phones is the desired outcome of billions of dollars of innovation; it is not just some random by-product of our interaction with tech. The internet and social media giants want control of our attention at all costs.

So where does this leave us?

From a personal perspective when we cannot attend to the person in front of us, it interrupts our capacity to connect. This in turn challenges the way we have always operated most successfully: as a tribe. From our very beginnings, we have relied on being part of a community, with different people allocated different roles, be they hunters, gatherers, nurturers, philosophers, healers, etc. Together as a group we were able to survive. When we repeatedly choose a device over a person, we risk disruption to the mechanism that has supported our very existence: connecting with others.

From a business perspective, this is diabolical news. At a bare minimum, most workplaces hope their people can pay attention to their work and get along with one another in the support of workplace goals. And while technology is implemented to get the job done faster, if its ultimate goal is to steal away our attention . . . then the actual impact of relying too heavily on tech is it lessening our capacity both to focus on the task at hand and to connect with others. From an organizational perspective, it does not leave us much to work with, so work is not working when tech addiction is in the building.

There are also other factors that workplaces need to consider: if tech addiction is impacting our focus and concentration, our intrinsic human problem-solving abilities become compromised. Over time, we forget that true innovation is the result of creative thinking, and our capacity to think outside of the box begins to atrophy—a situation that does not reflect the people we are on the inside and which certainly does not sound promising for our business prospects. And yet we continue to fall into the tech "rabbit hole." What I see time and again with technology is that it essentially delivers a false promise. For example:

- Technology promises to connect us, but it connects us without really allowing us to be "with" others. For example, it is estimated that up to 93 percent of our communication is nonverbal, and while our virtual world allows us to "see" people, we cannot see the full picture of them.

- Technology promises to make us smarter, but we know that multitasking is a myth, and the idea that we can really focus and pay attention to what we're doing when we are constantly being summoned by the pings on our phones or inboxes is farcical. When it comes to concentration, problem-solving, and innovation, technology is often an impediment to progress.

- Technology promises to save time, but many of us have also been in the position where we've responded quickly to a triggering email when we could have benefitted from picking up the phone or perhaps even arranging a meeting to discuss the issue. Now, that split-second reaction has landed us in hot water! It may have only taken ten seconds to reply, but it may take days, weeks, or months to undo the damage done to the relationship.

- Technology promises to be fun, but while social media and gaming and shopping apps promise entertainment, they also take us out of what is happening in our real lives. This prevents us from finding simple joy in our day-to-day. When I work with people, I ask them to consider mindful walking—not just walking to get from A to B, but taking time to look around and see what they see. I always love the conversations that come out of this, when people recount what they have been missing while they've been focused on the contents of their phones.

I think most of us recognize that technology often falls short of delivering on its promise, and yet, in many cases, we have become so reliant on (or even addicted to) technology that it feels like there's no turning back the digital clock.

Meanwhile, I also recognize that during the period of enforced lockdown, technology was what allowed me to keep my business running. Our consultants were able to reach out to people who were isolated without risking their own physical health to provide support in a time of enormous need. On a more personal level, it also allowed me to speak to my eighty-two-year-old mother ("face-to-face") each night. Even my daughter was able to share her latest slime production with her good friend Stella, at a time when they weren't able to meet in the school playground. But despite the enormous benefits of technology when it comes to staying connected with one another, our reliance on devices and automated systems at work comes at a great cost when we get the balance wrong.

And it seems we are doing exactly that. In 2011, the average American adult spent forty-five minutes a day on their phone. By 2021 that had ballooned to over four hours a day.[14] It is not at all surprising to me that in that same time frame, we also saw the mental health and loneliness epidemics soar—proof that these three "silent threats" to workplace well-being are all interconnected.

As we rebuild our workplaces in a post-COVID world, we need to ask ourselves: Where does technology help, and where does it hinder? Where does it *genuinely* assist in getting the job done, and how is this countered by the human cost of relying too heavily on tech? In essence, are we in charge of the technology that runs our businesses, or is it in charge of us?

Undoubtedly, the mental health epidemic, the loneliness epidemic, and the tech epidemic have each played a major (and often interlinked) role in how we have lost our way at work. As we move forward and rethink and rebuild our workplaces, we have the perfect opportunity to keep these factors front of mind while we are planning. In fact, address one of these elements well, and you will be taking steps to address them all.

Thinking more broadly, there is also an opportunity here for workplaces to actively contribute to improving public health *overall*. Many business owners may not feel that this is their responsibility or something that needs to be at the core of their business. But what I'm suggesting is that by looking away from the human issues impacting the people that make up your organization, you are also ultimately looking away from the overall success of your business as a player in the wider world.

When we establish systems in our workplaces that support people's health and well-being, we also do well as a business. This creates a ripple effect. When we have established practices and systems that allow our people to be seen, and for people to be connected and to be able recognize their contribution, those people go home with more energy, kindness, and generosity to extend to their families. In turn, their children show up at school the next day in a better space to learn, helping their teachers feel more appreciated and engaged in their work too. That teacher's family then reaps the rewards of this.

The knock-on effect for public health of people supporting people at work is so easy to see when we take a moment to look at the full picture—easier in a time when Zoom meetings have given us a window into peoples' homes and their lives outside the office. Work will work again when we are able to remember that the people we work with are whole human beings and when we are able to put models in place that support and empower them. Ultimately when people do well at work, they do well at home, and vice versa. Which is what I call a win-win.

.

# CHAPTER 2

# THE MAKING OF MAGIC

*Travelers, there is no path. Paths are made
by walking.*[1]
**—ANTONIO MACHADO**

**M**ost of us spend a lot of time at work. People often
refer to spending more hours with the people they
work with than they do with their family and friends. For
this reason, it has always made sense to me that if we are
genuinely interested in our health and well-being, then
addressing this in the workplace is the low-hanging fruit in
terms of having a real impact on our overall quality of life. If
this is where we spend the majority of our time (even when
it's virtual), then perhaps this is where we have the chance
to make the biggest difference when it comes to whether we
feel like we are winning at life. It is this thinking that led to
me discovering the foundations of MAGIC.

The therapeutic value of occupation has fascinated me
for over twenty-five years. This stems, first and foremost,
from my love of people's stories, the way you might think
you know someone and then they describe an experience

from their past and it allows you to see a whole different part of them. My husband says he thinks I have a sticker on my forehead that asks people to tell me all about their lives. But I'm just fascinated with the way a person has spent their time, the different life events and roads they have traveled as a result, and how this has shaped them.

Most of us have experienced those sliding-door moments when we've been able to feel a shift happening in our lives in real time. I experienced this when I was at university and my friend Heidi was interested in going to work in the USA after we graduated. I didn't think this was the path for me, but I went along with her to talk about opportunities in the States. Nine months later, it was me on the plane headed for Boston. By myself. In the meantime, Heidi had met her future husband and was no longer keen to go. Without a doubt, my time spent living and working in Boston shaped who I am today. As a new graduate, I got to work in a multidisciplinary and multicultural team. We had a physiotherapist from India, a physiotherapist from Holland, and a speech pathologist from Canada. This helped me realize that there was always more than one way of looking at things, an important lesson so early in my career. My roommates from that time, Meredith and Annmarie, are two of the people I still treasure most in my life. But perhaps most importantly, working in the United States also made me appreciate the free health care we have access to in Australia, which in itself gave me a profound understanding of the benefits and importance of preventative medicine.

If these sorts of life decisions can have such a lasting impact on who we are and the people we become, it makes sense that we pay attention to the ways in which we spend our days at work. This was true in the 1990s when I went to Boston, but I think it is even more relevant now. The ever-increasing influence of technologies designed to eat up our attention often prevents us from really paying attention to the small daily choices we are making. As much as big leaps can take us to all sorts of far-flung places, it's actually the micro-decisions about how we engage with daily life that can add up over time and have the biggest influence on how our lives play out. And given the amount of time and energy we put into our work, it makes sense that this area of life often has the biggest impact on who we are and how we live.

Over the years, I have seen people absolutely crushed by some of the choices they've made regarding their occupation, and I have equally seen others become absolutely exhilarated and captivated by the work they do every day. Most importantly, I have been witness to the precise circumstances that can create this kind of shift and the practices that can take a person from feeling as if they are sinking to a place where they are thriving. It's incredibly exciting to be a part of, and it's why I do what I do.

These days, we seem to be inundated with ways to improve our health and well-being, whether it's different ways of exercising or the latest superfood or supplement that will give us more energy and makes us feel better and brighter. But work—and how our mental, emotional, and physical well-being is impacted by where we work, the work we do, and the people we work with—is still a forgotten and often overlooked piece of the wellness puzzle. I'm not saying it's not important to focus on diet and exercise and their impact on well-being. We're learning so much more about how our bodies and brains work in tandem and how we can use this knowledge to support us. Let's spread the message far and wide! But haven't we also all sat and listened to a friend who feels their workload is out of control, or counseled a colleague during a period at work where they felt they were being bullied? Haven't we lived through one of these experiences ourselves? And haven't we seen the impact on life outside the office when things are not going well at work?

Going through a hard time at work can shift the equilibrium of a person's life in a way not many other things do. Left unchecked, this can create a ripple effect that engulfs everything. I see it happen in my practice all the time. It is not at all unusual for a client to share with me that aside from the problems they're experiencing at work, they also have serious physical health issues. It may be that they're taking medication to support their mental health or that their key relationships are in trouble. In order to avoid these scenarios, it's always made sense to me to focus on prevention—regardless of the level of free health care available. This means looking at what makes work *work*, by first and foremost asking the question, "What keeps people well at work?" By seeking to answer this, we have a chance to make an enormous impact on overall health and well-being, both for individuals who are struggling and for the people around them.

When statistics show us that 85 percent of people are not engaged at work, this feels more relevant than ever. With numbers like these, surely the only way is up! Imagining the possibilities if we could tweak this number just a fraction is what motivates me in my work—because I've also seen the *positive* ripple effect that results from people turning their workplace well-being around. When things are working at work again, people feel better about themselves and are happier overall. They are able to engage fully in all areas of their lives again. They describe changes such as no longer relying on wine to wind them down at night, resuming gardening on the weekends, or feeling up for exercise again. Most of all, they describe having more space in their lives for fun. Hallelujah to that! And this needn't mean turning everything upside-down and starting all over again. As somebody who has always believed that each individual has the power to change the course of our own destiny, I've also come to see the power and the potential of even the smallest shifts to positively impact our lives.

I love Bessie A. Stanley's thoughts on success. She writes:

> *To laugh often and much; to win the respect of intelligent people and the affection of children; to earn the appreciation of honest critics and endure the betrayal of false friends; to appreciate beauty, to find the best in others; to leave the world a bit better, whether by a healthy child, a garden patch, or a redeemed social condition; to know that even one life has breathed easier because you lived. This is to have succeeded.*[2]

While I feel my work definitely contributes to "redeemed social conditions," the line that really speaks to me is the one about knowing that "even one life has breathed easier because you have lived." I think we can get stuck on big ideas and grand gestures, but if at the end of the day your choices and actions have made one other person's life a little easier, then for me this is a life well lived. The issues we face as a society can feel overwhelming, and in the face of this it's easy to feel powerless or to become paralyzed. This means we end up feeling all the anxiety but not doing anything to address it. But with a simple reframe, a goal to make a difference to *one person's life* feels so much more possible. We begin to take action, the wheels are set in motion, and from there, who knows . . . it might not just be one life.

## WE ALL NEED A LITTLE MAGIC

While my career has given me ample opportunity to witness firsthand the positive impact that workplace well-being can have on people's lives, in more recent years I have begun to hear people speaking generally about work as something that only depletes us. This is undoubtedly due to the impact of the trifecta of factors discussed in the previous chapter: the epidemics of mental health, loneliness, and tech that have come to define working life in the early twenty-first century. When I began my practice in the 1990s, of course people had problems at work, but the escalation in workplace issues since then has been steep and unrelenting.

Thanks to the "always-on" nature of the modern working world, difficulties at work tend to follow us home with no clear boundary. This means there is no space for us to put the load down and reset at the end of each day. Over the past two decades, I have witnessed more and more people struggling at work—a downward spiral that led me to the realization that we absolutely could not keep working the way we've been working. The stories I was hearing in both my personal and my professional lives seemed more complex and more entrenched, and it was increasingly difficult to see the way through the problems people were describing. This realization is what started the train of thought that led to the development of the MAGIC framework.

It began with the need to get clear about what really makes work "work"—because I've seen firsthand that it can. Over the years, I had also studied reams of research telling us that when we are engaged with work in a positive way, it only supports our health and well-being. It was by digging deeply into this question that I came to identify the pillars that I have consistently seen make the most difference and have the most impact on people's lives. Let's recap on the pillars that inform the MAGIC framework and where they come from:

- **MEANING.** Having clarity around our values and knowing *why* we do what we do is a huge support to people when the going gets tough. This tethers us to something that matters, which is energizing both personally and professionally, particularly during the inevitable tough times at work. I think of finding meaning in your work as the through line that helps you stay connected to your place in the world and why you do the work you do.
- **AUTHENTICITY.** As a workplace mediator, I often help people navigate conflict in the workplace, and so often what's missing is that people feel they can't just "say what they mean." Constantly pushing down what's important to us and what we really want to say whittles away our confidence and self-belief, and this is a very dangerous downward spiral in terms of our overall health and well-being.
- **GROUND RULES.** With the pace of life only continuing to speed up, I have found myself focusing more and more on the principle of ground rules—that is, having a code of conduct we can keep coming back to. Neuroscience shows us that human beings crave a sense of certainty and that we need to feel as if we are in control of our lives. With so much in flux, there is huge value in finding even those small touch points that put you firmly in the driver's seat of life.
- **"I."** I've seen the difference in both my own team and the teams I work with when we take time to see the whole people that we work with—not just their professional output. This is because human beings connect with other human beings. Knowing the stories that make the person sitting next to you who they are

becomes the glue that holds a team together, making us more supportive of one another and more effective when it comes to achieving our collective goals.

- **CURIOSITY.** This final pillar stems from my having seen all the ways workplace communication can go awry. I'm often astounded by the assumptions we jump to and how quickly this can escalate workplace tensions. The simple act of *asking a question*, thus getting a better idea of what is going on for the other person, is nothing short of transformational. This is why I see curiosity as a superpower. In recent years, we have learned more about the brain and how it works, and I have seen how curiosity can help us sidestep the amygdala hijack—which throws us into fight-or-flight mode—while moving us toward greater understanding and collaboration—which is workplace gold.

When I first engaged with the process of identifying the factors I felt were most important when it came to workplace well-being, I was a little surprised and skeptical when I put it all together and came up with "MAGIC." *Really?* I thought. *I've built a business and reputation helping individuals and businesses to thrive at work, and the framework behind what I do is . . . MAGIC?* I questioned whether anyone would take me seriously. But the longer I sat with it, the more it made sense to me. Given the current state of play in our workplaces, a little MAGIC—that is, an approach that goes *beyond* facts and systems and data—is exactly what's needed.

We will explore each of the pillars outlined above more thoroughly throughout the next seven chapters in this book, where I've also included practical "workbook" sections for you to engage with them. For now, can you see what they have in common? Ultimately, the MAGIC framework is designed to bring some *humanity* back into the workplace. You might think of it as bringing both your head *and* your heart to work. We can puzzle our way mentally through a myriad of problems, but if we forget that our businesses are made up of human beings first and foremost, and if we can't prioritize taking care of these individuals, then we are in trouble.

It may be that you already feel you have some of these pillars covered in your workplace. For example, I work with lots of individuals and teams who are naturally great with ground rules, or who have worked hard to create a culture of "plain speak" so that people feel they have permission to speak freely and be heard in the workplace. But are people also being authentic at work? Have there been any big changes, either for the company or for them as individuals, that have shifted their concept of meaning? Certainly curiosity has been an essential component of trying to navigate a new road map forward in our post-pandemic world. No matter how good a workplace may be doing in any one of these areas, all the pillars of the MAGIC framework operating in tandem is what helps us stay open to the new while also keeping our footing on firm and stable ground.

Often, when the people and teams I work with come to me, all they know is that work isn't working—but they can't put their finger on why. In these instances, we will work through each of the five pillars of MAGIC to see what this uncovers. I'll be guiding you through this process throughout this book. And what it teases out is one essential truth when it comes to creating lasting, impactful change: *we need to be able to name things before we can change them.* Only once we know the exact nature of what needs to be addressed can we develop an action plan that is aligned with our goals and that will disrupt the workplace habits we have fallen into. This action plan will likely include some big-ticket items, but there will also be changes that can be implemented right away. As such, our work together here will go beyond the theory of workplace wellness; what you hold in your hands is a very practical manual that will provide a tangible strategy to improve the well-being of the people in your workplace.

More often than not, this does not mean reinventing the wheel. As I mentioned earlier, I strongly believe that the smallest changes can often have the biggest impact. For example, if a client tells me they're sleeping better, that they are worrying less about work on the weekends, or that they feel they are finally being heard by their supervisor, I see this as a *big* win. Why? Because this tells me that they are no longer on high alert, that adrenaline is not running the show, and that work is a place where they feel safe. It is operating from a constant state of hypervigilance, very common in the workplace of today, that I believe depletes us. When we're in this state at work, it's virtually impossible to shut off when we clock out, so we never get a chance to recover or recuperate before heading back in the next day. This cycle leaves us with nothing in the tank. At best, this impacts our performance on the job; at worst, it can lead to serious physical and mental health issues. But on the flipside, when teams tell me they are having more fun together, are better able to bounce back from difficulties, or feel more confident about approaching challenging conversations, I know that these seemingly "minor" shifts are a sign that work—and therefore everything else in their lives—is working again.

## MAGIC IN ACTION

So how does MAGIC work? The framework essentially asks you to humanize every aspect of your work culture, right from the recruitment stage. It then encourages you to make sure the people are front and center in your day-to-day working life, not just something you drop in and out of. For this reason, as simple as some of the practices may seem, working MAGIC requires commitment and consistency.

One of the strengths of viewing our working lives through the lens of occupational therapy (OT) is that a core skill of OT is to break the whole down into its parts in order to understand and improve the system. In seeing our people as *people* first and foremost, we begin to see occupation less as a daily slog to bring home the bacon and more as something that can *add* value and be therapeutic in and of itself. So often, when something isn't working, we try to look at the whole, but often this means we can't see the *trees* (the individuals involved) for the *forest* (the problem, whatever it is). In this case, we need to unravel it all and look a little closer. And this is what the MAGIC framework does. It breaks down "our work" into the components that impact the actual people doing the work, so that we can see clearly what's going well for them, what's not, and what we can adjust to make the whole system work again.

In addition to occupational therapy, I have trained in and used a number of models that have also contributed to the framework. Specifically, these are positive psychology, acceptance and commitment therapy, conflict coaching, mediation training, David Rock's SCARF model, and organizational mindfulness. All of these models focus on helping the human being first and foremost, so that people can thrive both as individuals and when working together as part of a wider system.

Dame Carol Black, the UK author of the 2008 workplace health report *Working for a Healthier Tomorrow*, was recently asked what makes the most difference when it comes to workplace health and well-being, to which she replied: "Please *do* put the fresh fruit and the bicycle schemes in, but please do not do it unless you've done leadership and stakeholder engagement and line manager capability [training]. Otherwise, it's a sticking plaster."[3] In this, she recognizes that we need a top-down, comprehensive, and consistent approach to addressing the issue of workplace well-being, where this becomes part of the culture and how the business is run.

It also means that *all* members of your workforce need to feel they are equipped to apply this approach. Let's face it; for most people, being asked to engage with and support other team member's physical and psychological health will see them navigating uncharted territory. They have likely been trained in how to complete a project, nail a brief, and deliver on a proposal. But ask them to learn how to look after their colleagues, or even to become aware of how they are managing in terms of their own well-being at work, and they will likely find themselves at a loss.

By acknowledging that the workplace has a fundamental role to play in an individual's health and well-being, we accept the responsibility (or perhaps the opportunity) to help all of our people flourish and thrive at work. In leaning into this, we are not only committing to a healthy workforce but are also contributing to broader public health and well-being. Given the fallout of the pandemic, for many of us this will hopefully feel like a timely commitment. Taking into account what we now know about the mental health and loneliness epidemics in particular, isn't it the right time to prioritize looking after one another?

In its essence, MAGIC is a framework and a blueprint

for sustainable living, both for organizations and the individuals that fuel them. By implementing this, we find ourselves traveling upstream, where we are better able to prevent people from "falling in the river." The framework is easy to action, and it will provide a foundation for the members of any workplace to keep referring back to as they take actions to change up tired old ways of doing things and breathe fresh life back into their workforce.

Of course, change will not happen overnight, and no one really knows what events we may need to respond to in the future. But we can use this framework to consider each step forward, one interaction at a time, asking ourselves if it moves us closer to or further away from connecting with our people—as a means of both supporting them as individuals and meeting our wider business goals. The MAGIC tricks outlined in this book are designed to give us areas to focus on, right here and right now, as well as a road map to keep coming back to while we are in the process of rebuilding—for the benefit of us all going forward.

## A PERSONAL INTEREST

Beyond my professional experience in the field, I have also benefited firsthand from a more human approach to work. As I have already outlined, I first studied occupational therapy over twenty-five years ago, and as a result I have always had a keen interest in the link between how we occupy our time and our overall health and well-being. But my own family history has also demonstrated to me, in a very real way, the difference workplace well-being can have on an individual's life and the wider repercussions of this for future generations.

My paternal grandmother, Florence Darmody, was eight months pregnant with her fifth child when her thirty-five-year-old husband, Bill, was taken to a hospital in a regional town in Queensland to have his appendix taken out. While there, Bill contracted sepsis, and he never returned home. At the time he was a railway master. In this role, he had traveled throughout the state, as country service was a fundamental part of the job. Of course, his family also traveled around the state with him, with all the children apart from two having been born in different towns.

So what was Flo, his widow, to do? She had five children to feed and no income, and there were certainly no single-mother benefits in those days. So she wrote to Queensland Rail. She outlined her husband's service, explaining that she, as his spouse, had also traveled throughout Queensland and, in doing so, supported the company. She then asked for a position to keep this Queensland Rail family afloat—ideally, taking into account her husband's dedicated years of country service, a Brisbane posting so that she could be closer to her siblings. Flo certainly understood the importance of community, not only within the Queensland Rail family; being close to her brothers and sisters was also a priority if this family of four boys and one girl, all under the age of ten, was going to thrive.

In response to her request, Queensland Rail came through, providing her with a post as railway master for Bald Hills railway station in Brisbane. She stayed in this job for twenty years. Most importantly, this role included the station house, which became the family home. It was positioned next to the station, so while Flo had to be at work at 4:30 a.m., she could still monitor the comings and goings of the household and maintain some modicum of order (as best you can with five children) as the matriarch of the family.

It's a story that reads like a bit of a fairy tale, especially given the instability of many workplaces now. And I recognize that it might be difficult to replicate this extraordinary level of support today—market instability, the rise of the gig economy, and increased competition means jobs that can provide this level of support are few and far between. But nonetheless, I have always applauded Queensland Rail for seeing Flo as a human being, and recognizing her human needs, first and foremost. Who knows what would have happened to this family without their support. With their mother in a steady job and with a stable home base for their development, Flo's five children all made their way in the world. Perhaps not surprisingly, many of them also sought out careers that in some way "redeemed social conditions": my father, aunt, and uncles went on to work in social work, psychology, and public service, and one of them operated a small hardware store that was a hub for the local community. With this story in my background, it has always been crystal clear that humanizing the workplace changes lives.

If you're a manager, how might your workplace contribute to this positive-feedback loop, were you to look first and foremost toward your people and see them for who they are and what they need versus simply automatons who perform a certain role for you? If you're part of a team, how could the place you work provide more support for your life outside the office? When considering these deep questions about the real role of our occupations in our lives, it could be that MAGIC will make all the difference.

As I mentioned, many of the teams and individuals I work with do not need to work on all aspects of MAGIC. When I begin a new project, I will make enquiries rooted in each of the different aspects of the model, allowing people ample space to describe their experiences to me. Based on this initial assessment, I'm able to provide feedback on the areas I think we need to focus on. In some cases, this might lead to a complete systems overhaul. But more often than not, it will mean implementing small changes and shifts in habits and behaviors that can have a profound impact over time. Having worked with people for so long, I know when things are working when there's a shift in what I call the "temperature" of a workplace. I can feel it as soon as I walk through the door, and I can see it in the smiles on people's faces. When work starts to work again, it becomes a place where people want to be.

# CHAPTER 3

# MEANING

The MAGIC framework begins with finding meaning, and this is where we must begin on our journey to making work work again. As leadership expert Simon Sinek puts it so succinctly, "Start with the why." So let's begin by looking at the importance of the why in the workplace.

The WorkHuman Research Institute's 2017 report, *Bringing More Humanity to Recognition, Performance, and Life at Work*, found that having a personal sense of meaning in one's work life was even more important to respondents than compensation (salary, benefits, and other perks), which ranked as the third most important reason for staying in a job. Interestingly, they found that there is very little difference for employees between having no recognition program at all and having one that is not tied to a company's core values.[1]

This would suggest that time spent talking up packages and perks—whether you're the employer or the employee—is taking us down the wrong path. Of course, everybody wants to be well compensated for the work they do, and the better the benefits, the better looked-after we feel. But if this isn't married with an intrinsic sense of why we do the work we do, it leaves us with an emptiness, a void that no number of perks can fill. In fact, among those I work with, it's often the people with the most perks who seem to be the unhappiest—an indicator perhaps that their workplaces have focused more on the "bells and whistles" and have not really taken the time to consider why they do what they do. They believe success is more about how it looks to the outside world, rather than how it feels on the "inside."

Sadly, meaning is often an afterthought. For example, could you confidently name, right now, the deeper meaning of the work you do? How about the company or clients you work for? I am always interested to hear what people say when I ask about the meaning behind their work, and I find it curious that often people have not given it much thought. Conversely, for those who have, I love seeing how much conviction and confidence this brings them, as if they have found their purpose; they are clear about why they get up in the morning.

For those who know exactly why they do the work they do, I have also seen how this helps them weather the storms that are an inevitable part of life. As Nietzsche said, "He who has a why to live can bear almost any how."[2] You wouldn't start a big DIY project or embark on a new course of study without a clearcut why, so doesn't it also make sense to be clear about your reasons for doing the work you do, whether this means why you are pursuing your chosen career, why you work for the company you do, or why you're committed to a certain project? And beyond having a clear-cut goal or objective, the meaning in MAGIC is also about understanding how your contribution makes a difference—not only to the world but in terms of who you are.

It's a distinction that often gets lost when the focus is simply on getting the job done, ideally as cheaply as possible. But we lose so much when we forget to include meaning in our preparation process. I often liken this to planning a big vacation. If you don't know what kind of break you need, how can you even choose a location? Let alone start booking planes, trains, and ferries to get you there. You also won't be able to plan for the activities that will provide the enjoyment and make it all worthwhile. Without a clear why, you could very well end up on a busy city trip when your body was craving a week on the beach. In this scenario, you may end up traveling home more exhausted than when you left, and we all know how frustrating that is.

It's understandable why meaning often gets left on the shelf. The pace of the world we're living in often leads us to jump in, quickly get to the finish line, and move on to the next project. But taking time to reflect on our why does not need to be a lengthy process. In my coaching sessions, it often only takes a few minutes for a person to recognize why they do what they do—which often leads to a deeper realization about how they have ended up where they are. Sometimes it is directly related to the work itself and the product or services they are providing, and other times it is rooted in the company culture and values; we feel drawn to a company that values quality service and respecting others, or where a focus on worker health and well-being leads to flexible working arrangements that allow people to care for themselves as they take care of business. By being overt about what our work means to us in the context of our wider lives, we are able to clarify our purpose. We begin to remember that we are active participants in our own lives, and this feels good! Especially in a world where it can often feel as if life is happening to us.

And while it's one thing to get clear about our why as individuals, it is also important to understand our why as a team. If we're working in a team and we have not taken the time to figure this out as a group, then we can have people headed in different directions, taking different planes, trains, and ferries to get there. While the project might have a clear objective, behind the scenes there is chaos. It may not be self-evident, but until everybody is on the same ship, you will find yourselves constantly course correcting, a trajectory as chaotic as it is exhausting.

And why should we expect it to be smooth sailing if it's not crystal clear where we're headed and why we're headed there? Think about your current workplace. What is your why for what you do? Is this something you discuss regularly with your colleagues? Do you think they feel the same as you? What does a good year look like for you on a personal level? What about a good week, or even a good day? Do these answers come easily to you, or is it all a bit blurry?

In a post-COVID world, there is no room for blurry. With so much uncertainty in the world, it's more important than ever to get clear on where we are headed and to understand the deeper why behind what we do. As we rebuild our workplaces together, the ones that thrive will be the ones that can picture and describe the meaning that underpins their mission in detail. Only with this in place will the people joining the journey feel supported and stable. Not only this, but they will also be motivated to get fully on board and to stay the course when things get rocky. And if there was ever a time when we needed all hands on deck to navigate the path forward, it's now.

## *Writing It Out:*
### THE POWER OF JOURNALING

While considering our why, and throughout the following chapters on how to implement the principles of MAGIC, I'll be suggesting journaling exercises as a means of getting under the "monkey mind" and down to what's happening on a deeper level. The monkey mind is that unsettled part of the brain that often feels like it's running the show with its constant chatter. It can be quite distracting and mischievous and can take us down paths that are not helpful. Ideally, when considering the wider arc of our work and our lives, we want to be able to choose our thoughts—not the other way around. Journaling allows us to get our thoughts out of our heads and on to paper, giving us the opportunity to then have a really good "look" at exactly what we are thinking.

So often after a journaling exercise, clients will tell me: "I can't believe that was running around in my head!" Finally, they can see the extent to which their thoughts have taken hold and the power their thoughts have wielded in their lives. With them down on paper, they are able to get some clarity, along with a better understanding of what is actually true for them and what really matters.

So how to actually get started? Journaling is sometimes described as the activity of "free writing." You can start by just writing whatever thoughts are going through your mind or by using a prompt such as "How can I be my best self today?" Or you might think of an issue that is current for you and write about that. I always suggest putting a timer on. It can be easy to think you're "done" after jotting down the first stream of thoughts, but pushing through at this point and writing for five minutes or more is often what leads to the real nuggets of gold.

If you stall, simply pause and then keep writing down whatever arises next in your mind. It might be that you are finding journaling annoying! But please stick with it. Journaling can be used to uncover deeper aspects of our lives that often get lost in the busyness of the day-to-day, and it will certainly be a valuable tool as we proceed with looking for the MAGIC in our workplaces.

## THE MAGIC OF MEANING

In a study that was carried out in a psychiatric unit in Vancouver in 1989, professor Michael Chandler discovered that very depressed people have become disconnected from a sense of the future, in a way that other very distressed people have not.[3] This demonstrates just how important it is to have a clear vision of where we want to go and why we want to go there. Given that, for many of us, work plays such a big part in our lives, being disconnected from the meaning of our work can clearly have a significant impact.

Earlier, we explored research that shows how, when done well, work can support our mental health—while we are also in the grips of a mental health epidemic. Chandler's research highlights one way in which we are going wrong. By jumping into a job or a project without first getting aligned on the deeper meaning behind our work, we are bypassing an important part of what makes our work worthwhile. When we're connected to meaning, the inevitable struggles and challenges we all face from time to time become easier to manage.

Gaining clarity around our meaning, and mapping out our future at work, whether as an individual or as part of a team, is a fundamental aspect to supporting good mental health in the workplace. We know from neuroscience that our brains crave certainty—something that has become a rare commodity in our fast-paced world. But simply getting clear about our meaning can provide some of the steadiness that we crave. Some people describe our current working conditions as VUCA: Volatile, Uncertain, Complex, and Ambiguous. If this is the case, we need the constant of meaning more than ever. Remember how I have my clients imagine standing in the middle of a seesaw, and how exhausting this can be? Understanding meaning provides one of the blocks that can steady us—even more essential when we also consider that Google's Project Aristotle identified psychological safety as the most important factor for a successful team. Following the unprecedented changes of 2020, we are craving security and stability more than ever. Beyond financial security, what might this look like in your workplace or for you as an individual?

Simply put, meaning means understanding the "big picture" of the work you do, which in turn becomes the foundation for all you are building. When completing a jigsaw puzzle, we constantly check in with the "big picture" on the box to get our bearings and to confirm we are on track. Imagine how much more difficult and frustrating it would be to be working away at something with no reference point for what you are working toward.

Now consider this in relation to your workplace. What are you and your team working toward? Have you been shown the big picture, or are you just expected to work away on your small piece of the puzzle? If it is the latter, can you get a sense of how destabilizing this can be? Without knowing the broader impact of your output, not only in terms of productivity but also on the wider world, it is as if you are adrift on a raft out at sea.

But if you draw a blank when it comes to meaning, where are you even supposed to start? Even the word itself can feel a little overwhelming. But finding meaning doesn't have to take over your life with a big roar; it can manifest as a very quiet determination. So let's break it down into smaller steps and look at the different aspects of what makes up meaning to you.

This begins with considering the values of your organization, your team, and yourself as an individual. What is important to you; what is your true north? Then—and this is what makes the difference—consider how this looks in your day-to-day. How would you know you and your team were living by your values; what would you be seeing? The next step is to look at how people are being rewarded for living these values. It can be disheartening to see people being rewarded for actions that seemingly go against the values of an organization. Imagine how good it would feel to turn this around.

You can also ask your team what success looks like from a more holistic perspective. Again, in today's world, we are so focused on productivity that we often neglect to recognize what is working well on a more human level. Stopping to pay attention to this gives us clarity about what is really important to us, which can lead to an understanding of what provides us with meaning. Start with exploring what a "big win" would look like, and then perhaps a successful week, even down to a successful day. What you come up with will provide clues as to what holds significance in the workplace for you. Perhaps a good day is when everyone gets together for lunch, when someone sends a congratulatory email, or when you are able to leave work on time. Beyond our output, we are looking at what makes us *feel good* at work; when we uncover this, we will be able to make work work better.

Knowing who you want to be, knowing what you do well, and being able to identify what would constitute a "win" can all help us to get a better idea of what work means to us. Let's dig into these questions a little deeper.

## ✳ *Workbook*

Throughout the following chapters, you will find lots of practical exercises providing the prompts that will help you to uncover what the MAGIC is for you. I would suggest keeping a journal handy so you can keep a record of what you find along the way.

1.  What are your organization's values?

2.  How do you see these values being lived out in your organization? Give five recent examples of this.

3.  How are people recognized and rewarded for living these values? For example, we end our staff meetings by getting people to nominate their colleagues for actions that supported our organization's values; what could you do?

4.  If there was a question that you could ask in an interview that would help you to determine whether the person across the table from you has the same values as your company, what would it be? At my workplace, integrity is one of our values. We ask everyone applying for a position, "When has your integrity been challenged, and what did you learn about yourself when it was?"

5. What does success look like for you and for your team beyond "the work"? Break it down, and include answers for the following: a big win, a successful week, a successful day.

## WHAT ARE MY VALUES?

As I touched on above, even the word "meaning" can be intimidating for people. With so much to juggle in our day-to-day, how are we supposed to find the headspace to think about the big picture? But I'm not out to make anybody feel guilty here. Given that aligning your personal sense of meaning with the work that you do is often the key to workplace well-being, I want to show you how simple it can be to do this.

We can begin to make the question of meaning more manageable by considering our values: what I care about, who I want to be, and what success looks like for me. Naming these things brings us closer to our meaning. Knowing our values can also help us to feel connected to our future goals and more stable on a path, as if we have our feet firmly on the ground. It can also allow us to make decisions based on where we actually want to go, bringing us closer to what's important to us or helping us to notice where we have turned away from what matters.

If work isn't working, chances are there is a discrepancy between our values and the work that we do, which is in fact a fairly easy problem to solve if we're able to simply quit our jobs and find others that are a better fit. What's a bigger problem is when our actions and the ways we are living our lives are not aligned with our own values. If this is the case, our dissatisfaction with work will follow us from job to job. The internal conflict that arises when we are disconnected from our meaning can also be excruciating. It's not quite so easy to "quit" ourselves, although we see this played out throughout numbing behaviors that are on the increase.

So let's take a look at where there may be a values gap in your life.

## ✳ Workbook

1. What are your top three values? Mine are courage, kindness, and connection. If you're finding this question hard to answer, take a look at the list of common values on my website. When doing this exercise, I really encourage you to go with your gut feeling about what your core values might be; sometimes you just know.

2. How can you see your values at play in your life? Write down five scenarios where you felt you were living out your values, the things you hold dear. Alternatively, is there a time you felt you weren't living aligned with your values? What happened, and what did you learn about yourself?

3. What does a successful day and a successful week look like for you?

4. What are the achievements that you are most proud of? Make a list of at least ten. This might also provide some clues about what is important to you.

If you haven't considered the deeper meaning of your life before, these kinds of questions will begin to help you begin to uncover the things that really matter to you. As you work through these questions, remember that there are no wrong answers; we're all different, aren't we? Finding your meaning is about celebrating what makes us different, rather than trying to squash your magnificent square peg into a round hole. Please also remember to be kind with yourself. There have undoubtedly been times when you did not live out your values, and that's okay; we've all been there. Rather than beat yourself up, see this as an opportunity to simply become more aware of your actions so you are better able to align them with your values in the future.

## MAKING TIME FOR WHAT MATTERS

In a world with so many distractions and so many competing demands, it has never been more important to focus on how we occupy our time. If we are going to lead meaningful lives, we need to be aware of where our time is going. We all recognize that we spend a lot of time at work, and many of us often joke about our "work wives" or "work husbands," as we see more of them than we do our families. But as a workplace mediator, I can tell you that when things go south at work, this is never contained to the office. Problems at work can see people losing sleep, being snappy at home, and even becoming physically unwell. If things can affect us to this extent when they are going badly, let's just imagine what the impact could be when they are going well.

This concept has never been a stretch for me; in fact it's pretty much what brings meaning to *my* work. I am driven by the idea that the way we occupy our time has the capacity to have a therapeutic effect.

When it literally comes down to how we spend the hours in our day, I also know there are lots of aspects to our work lives over which we have no control. We can't always determine our workloads or what resources we have to get the job done. Perhaps it's impossible to see the deeper meaning to it all. But it is always possible to become a more active participant in how we live out our days.

I am pretty sure most of us don't get up in the morning with the following goals for our time:

- I plan to spend as much time on social media and the internet as possible today.
- I plan to be distracted and not really listen to my daughter today.
- I plan to check my phone twenty to fifty times every hour.
- I plan to multi-screen through most of my day.
- I plan to write an obnoxious email to my work colleague.
- I plan to walk past people without acknowledging them because I am concentrating on my phone.

We may not set out with these intentions, but this can often be how our day ends up, leading to us feeling a little lost and empty. Deep down, we know that we didn't end up where we wanted to. How differently would your days play out if you proactively applied some meaning to the way you spend your time? Let's take a look.

## ❋ Workbook

1. Choose one aspect of your day where you would like to begin living in a way that you can see is aligned to your values. Here are some ideas:

   - If you value connection, you might really listen to a colleague with a problem rather than zoning out or jumping in prematurely with what you want to say.
   - If you value health and well-being, you might address

that 3:00 p.m. lull with a walk around the block to wake yourself up rather than reaching for the sugar.

- If you value innovation, you might make a pact with yourself to ask more questions in a meeting instead of pretending you know it all.
- If you value kindness, you might become more aware of your colleagues' moods and offer a coffee or a chat where you can see it is needed.
- If you value recognition, you might send a surprise email to a colleague patting them on the back.

2. Identify your default zone; when do you notice yourself sleepwalking through your life? What could you do to change this behavior and be more engaged in every moment?

3. How does your workplace encourage people to stay engaged? Are phones banned from meetings? Do you have a policy around after-hours emails that gives people permission to be more present at home? What could your workplace do to make sure people are a little more available to what is in front of them?

---

After working through this section, you should hopefully have a list of practical ways to make sure that meaning is front and center in your life. Pick one or two of these ideas, and create a plan for the coming week; how can you make more time for what really matters? At the end of the week, you can do some journaling and reflect on how this worked out for you.

## MINDFULNESS: IF NOT NOW, THEN WHEN?

Living with meaning and becoming aware of how we are spending our days means being mindful of our actions—a concept that is rapidly gaining traction. In an age of mass distraction, living on autopilot has become the norm, and it makes sense that thought leaders and business gurus alike are singing the praises of mindfulness. It is often presented alongside meditation, and I understand that it may not be for everyone. But when you strip it down to basics, mindfulness is simply the practice of *paying attention* to how we are living.

Without this, is it any wonder we get to the end of the workday, week, or year and are unable to really identify how we contributed, what we achieved, and what any of it meant to us? By incorporating mindfulness into our working lives, we are also supporting ourselves and our colleagues to step out of the adrenaline-fueled fog that permeates many a workplace and into a space of conscious decision-making.

So how can you implement a program that encourages people to reengage with their day-to-day without them being put off by the term "mindfulness"? Or engage in this practice yourself without drawing judgment from skeptical colleagues? Given how much we now know about the benefits of mindfulness for individuals, teams, and organizations alike, how do we entice those who are saying "thanks but no thanks" and make mindfulness available and accessible to everyone?

As a coach, I know that this can be as simple as getting people to stop, breathe into their bellies, and really feel into their bodies, even if it's just for a moment. I have yet to meet a single person who doesn't concede that they feel a little better taking a minute out of their day for this, for simply paying attention to how they are feeling and coming back into the present. Get a person to try this, and they have dipped a toe into mindfulness without even realizing it.

In truth, mindfulness can be as simple as five minutes of journaling; taking a walk around the block where you notice all the sights, sounds, and smells; or tuning in to really listen to what a person is saying. The secret lies in learning how to grab opportunities to pause during the day.

Certainly, an exercise in "mindful listening" always creates a lot of discussion in the workplace. When we encourage people to just listen for two minutes to their partners—not asking questions, not adding their insights, just listening—it becomes immediately clear how this is often missing from their daily interactions. They often describe "hearing more detail" or "understanding more of what the person was saying." Most people leave this exercise thinking not only about how it has changed the quality of their interactions with their teammates but also how they could use this in their home lives.

When the workplace starts being described as VUCA (Volatile, Uncertain, Complex, and Ambiguous), is it any wonder that we've learned to respond to issues from our amygdala, the part of the brain that triggers the fight-or-flight response? But while this kind of reaction is vital in the path of an oncoming car, living from this place is the fast track to making ill-considered decisions that get us nowhere. If we want a life with meaning, we need to be able to consider what choices we can make today that will set us up for longer term "success" (whatever that looks like to us). Mindfulness can bring us out of this part of our brain that reacts emotionally and into the part of our brain that allows us to respond. If you are wanting to run the show, then mindfulness will help you to be an active participant in your life. Let's look at three things we do at work every day and explore how we turn these into "mindfulness practices"—so even the naysayers can get on board!

## ✳ *Workbook*

### MINDFUL RESET

A mindful reset can prevent you from tumbling through the day at a cracking pace, and it's something I use all the time. Each time I sit at my workstation, I feel my bottom on the chair, I feel my back against the backrest, and I feel my feet on the floor. I find this simple exercise gets me out of the chatter in my head and back into the present moment—which is the only place where I can actually get any work done! Another client of mine takes a deep breath every time they walk through a doorway; you can imagine how many times a day they then get to "reset." Another client puts his hand on his chair each time he enters a meeting and silently wishes the best for all involved—a far better way of kicking things off than imagining all the things that could go wrong! Often, all we need is a small cue that reminds us to get out of our ruminations about the past or our worries for the future and back into the present. Many of my clients have a visual reminder on their desktop to take a deep breath into their belly (no one else needs to know what it is for)—and sometimes that is all it takes.

### MINDFUL WALKING

I think most people can see that walking is a fundamental part of their workday—even if it's just walking from their car to their office or from their desk to the bathroom. The first place to start when transitioning to mindful walking is to not be looking at your phone! But there also are a number of ways we can make this everyday work activity even more mindful, including:

- Really ground into your feet. Feel your left foot touch the ground, then feel your right, then feel your left, then feel your right, and continue feeling them each time each foot hits.

- Focus on your breath. Anytime you're walking from A to B, take this opportunity to make sure you are really breathing deeply into your belly and not just into your chest. This will elicit a relaxation response in the parasympathetic nervous system. Imagine actually encouraging relaxation when heading from meeting to meeting, rather than getting into your head about what you have or haven't managed to get done. Which will set you up for a better outcome?

- Notice your surroundings. Simply looking around and noticing your environment is a mindful walking practice. Set a goal to notice five blue things, to count the number of signs you see, or to tally how many people walk past you wearing red. It's always interesting to do this exercise in places that are very familiar. I've worked in the same building for eighteen years and lived in the same house for thirteen years, and I am always surprised by the things I notice when I really focus on what is "out there," rather than the chatter in my head!

What can mindful walking achieve? It can be an opportunity to reset between meetings, an opportunity to regroup after a nasty email, or an opportunity to recharge—all these benefits and no extra time out of your day!

## MINDFUL EATING

Last but not least, mindful eating is my very favorite mindfulness practice. Again, hopefully eating is already part of your workday. But how many times have you finished eating something and realized that you can't remember actually tasting it? We often eat our lunch while reading emails, and I get that you might not have time for a long lunch. But all I am suggesting is to focus on the first three bites of a sandwich or the first three sips of tea. Just note the taste, the texture, and the aroma of what you're eating. In the five to ten seconds this takes, we can come back into the present and have the chance to reset. I know a team that has a mindful lunch once a week. Perhaps you could start your day by having a mindful breakfast. Maybe try it out with the family to start everyone's day in a positive way. I always enjoy trying out mindful eating with groups. We usually have a variety of things to eat, and there is always lots of chatter; often people say things like:

"I didn't realize I was such a noisy eater."
"I hadn't noticed how sweet this is."
"I can't believe how quickly I usually eat without noticing anything."

This is a great intro exercise to try out with a team, but again, once you know what to do, it takes no extra time out of your day—though you may want to try out the mindfulness practice of one of my past clients: after a particularly tough day, she would have a piece of chocolate mud cake and savor every single bite.

Again, I really encourage you to take small steps and just choose one activity and try it out for a week. You might find at the end of the week it did not work for you at all, which will allow you then to recognize that it is not for you and to try something else for another week.

## A JOY TO WORK WITH

*Joy collected over time fuels resilience.*[4]

**—BRENÉ BROWN**

Most workplaces have rolled out resilience training. They have ticked that box. Certainly, leadership is crying out for a more "resilient" workforce. People who can "bounce back" are what every employer wants. But if this is the case, what are we also doing to *collect joy*? Brené Brown's quote suggests that if we really want to "stop people from falling in the river," more joy at work might be just what we need.

But how often is joy even on the agenda? Especially if the goal of your workplace is simply for people to come in, keep their nose to the grindstone, and just make it through the day. During COVID, when I asked people what they missed about the office, they often described laughs with a colleague, walking to get coffee, or a trivia night with the team. It was the moments of joy. It became clear that beyond "getting the job done," these moments were the glue that held everything together in the places where work was really working.

The first step to bringing joy back to your workplace is to figure out what this might mean to your team. After all, everyone finds joy in different places, don't they? One team I work with plays soccer once a week at lunchtime. One of the teams I coach does jigsaw puzzles and frames them. At my own workplace, we have a team member who likes to write poetry, and we all wait for the next installment of that teammate's work, eager to see how we each feature.

Given the pressure of the workplace today, the days where the odd morning tea or birthday cake could fulfill our need for joy are long gone. What's needed to balance out the epidemics of mental health, loneliness, and tech addiction (which are often rife in our places of work) and to help us back into meaning and real resilience is a robust "joy program" that speaks individually to the people on your team. As leaders, it is on us to fill the joy void. It's a cop-out to put joy in the "too hard" basket or to label it "too warm and fuzzy." If you really want your people to go the extra mile, joy must be on the agenda.

A joy program might mean creating a "wall of wins" on a big noticeboard in your office, where you use Post-it Notes to record all the things that have been going well. (A team that I work with used this during a significant period of change, and they were surprised at how many things went well with the change process when they looked at the board. They all recognized that the only things that kept playing through their minds were the things that had not worked out.) A joy program might also be two minutes at the beginning of the team meeting to talk about what brings the team members alive. It might be a commitment to journaling about joy, or maybe it's an afternoon of lawn bowls, a trivia night, a book club, a group jigsaw puzzle, or a corporate cooking class. I don't know what joy means for your team. Do you?

Joy also needs to be part of the conversation at work. It should be discussed during recruitment ("What brings you joy?"), as well as during a new employee's induction ("We value joy here; we think it helps to make us more resilient. What puts the joy in your life?") When you realize someone might be having a tough time, do you talk to them about how they might find some time for joy in their day? I'm always saddened by the people who have given no thought to joy in their working week or who rely on a Friday-night blowout in the pub to find joy—even when the hangover impacts their enjoyment of rest of the weekend.

We sometimes tend to think joy "just happens." As if we'll just find ourselves having fun at some point. But the reality is that joy needs to be scheduled, just like everything else in the busy lives we lead today. If joy truly is the fuel of resilience, then in a post-pandemic world it should absolutely be on the agenda. In fact, it probably should be the number one item.

## ✳ *Workbook*

1. What brings you joy?

2. When was the last time you experienced joy at work?

3. What could your team do to put joy back on the agenda?

4. Does your recruitment process include questions that ask people how they have fun? A strong answer to this question may suggest a resilient person is sitting in front of you.

5. How could you explore what joy means for each person at your workplace? If you want to genuinely get to know a person, knowing what lights them up is certainly a great start!

As you are beginning to see, when something "just does not feel right," whether at work or in a person's life in general, reconnecting to the meaning behind it all is a great place to start. Getting clear on this means first and foremost stopping to take stock, as we really arrive in our life, and ask the question: "What is important to *me*, and how can I make space for more of this in my life?" If we want work to work again, then we need to know what the goal of it all is. Many of us have been living our lives on autopilot, and becoming aware of our meaning allows us to take back the controls and become active participants in our own lives once more. Now that we're back in the driver's seat, let's move on to look at the role authenticity plays in bringing back the MAGIC to the workplace.

# CHAPTER 4

# AUTHENTICITY

In his outstanding book *Lost Connections*, Johann Hari describes a common symptom of depression called "derealization," a state in which you feel like nothing you are doing is authentic or real.[1] To feel we can "be ourselves," be real, and be accepted just as we are is powerful—but sadly it is also pretty rare. And just as feelings of derealization can be a symptom of depression, living what might be called an authentic life can support our mental health. This translates to the workplace in a number of ways.

For example, think of someone who loves you unconditionally, just the way you are. Perhaps close your eyes and picture this person in front of you. How does it feel? Most people I do this exercise with describe feeling warm, secure, safe, or joyful. Now imagine turning up at your workplace feeling this way each day. Alternatively, feeling that you are not accepted as you are can lead to you constantly doubting yourself, to the point it almost feels like you are under attack. In this state, our adrenaline starts pumping, a visceral, chemical response that impacts our focus, our interactions with others, and our capacity to weigh the consequences of our decisions, to name just a few effects. Not the ideal state of mind to be approaching your working day. It's also exhausting to feel you have to "keep up appearances" in order to fit in. Simply put, if we are serious about supporting worker health and well-being, we need to actively promote authenticity in the workplace. But what does this mean, and where do we start?

Firstly, we need to understand what it is to be authentic. The definition given in the *Oxford English Dictionary* is "to be genuine, not a copy of."[2] So often in the working world, we have an idea of what we *think* we need to bring to our job, whether this relates to the expectations of our role as a manager or the values we perceive as being aligned with the company we work for. But if the actions we perform and the beliefs we operate under are not aligned with who we are as people, authenticity is eroded. We might think we're performing in a way that's expected of us, or that will guarantee our success, but we're no longer being genuine. We have become a "copy" of an idealized employee we *think* will get ahead.

Being authentic, being real, means being able to bring your whole self to work, including your beliefs, the things you care about, your way of doing things, and the stories that make you you. Most of all, it means not selling out on those things that matter the most to you. For me, there is no "work Sharon" and "home Sharon." I am simply Sharon, no matter what "role" I am performing, be it boss, therapist, coach, or mother. No matter what situation I am in, my priorities—investing in people, finding connection, and practicing kindness, to name a few—the things that give my life *meaning*, are consistent.

Of course, most workplaces require some degree of compromise when it comes to how we behave and the systems within which we perform our duties. We also all have different needs, and no one workplace can be expected to accommodate each and every nuance of our personal preferences. But in order to create and foster a culture of authenticity, and to prevent people from becoming disconnected from our wider mission, we need to be crystal clear as individuals and as a company about what the big-ticket items are for us and where we will not budge without selling ourselves out. Beyond our goals as a company, understanding who we are and living according to these values is one way to achieve inner and outer stability—something we are all craving in these times of uncertainty. Living in alignment with our values becomes a solid foundation we can rely on when things get rocky. Can you feel the truth in this? Seen this way, authenticity is one way to steady the seesaw and find inner and outer stability.

One thing that undermines authenticity is the game playing and political maneuvering that seems to be embedded in so many workplaces. I've seen so many teams marred by a culture of competitive point scoring, where people feel they have to outperform one another (literally). But if you want people to be straight with you and not play games, you have to be real with them. Are you ready for that? This is not a trick question. Given that game playing is something most of us detest and feel is a complete waste of time, it's important that we all reflect on how straight we're prepared to be with people—especially if it means being the one to "go first." It takes courage and conviction to drop the bravado and consistently show up as our true selves. Most of us like to be liked. We also want to seem like we have all the answers and that others can rely on us. But valuing being liked over being ourselves is a dangerous game. "Playing to the crowd" versus risking being unpopular leads to empty promises and dismissals of uncomfortable truths; before long, what's really important—to us as individuals and to the success of our teams—becomes eroded.

This is especially destabilizing during times when we feel we have very little control over events in the outside world, something we have all been confronted with in the era of COVID. But being brave enough to be real, to be vulnerable, and to begin fostering a culture of authenticity actually helps us feel more in control. The more you "fake it until you make it," the more you end up second-guessing yourself and even questioning what's "real." And honestly, who's got the time and energy for that, especially with so much in flux in the wider world? On the flip side, being authentic allows you to feel more self-assured, more trusting, and more centered. Our brains crave certainty—in fact, a way of looking at anxiety is simply our minds trying to find something to cling to. But it's when we settle on what is "certain" for us, and start making choices and taking actions in alignment with this, that things begin to settle and we are able to feel a little more comfortable in our own heads.

This is especially important for anybody who finds themselves in a leadership position. As we begin to rebuild our working lives in the wake of 2020, many of us will be returning to the workplace feeling a little battered and bruised and looking for leaders we can depend on. And no matter how convincing the "front," we can tell when we're being lied to. It's something we feel in our bones, even if confused minds are easily manipulated by confident (if inauthentic) rhetoric. Authentic leadership, meanwhile, means letting people know exactly who you are (weaknesses, doubts, and all), what you believe, and what you can offer people consistently from day to day.

Let's explore the concept a little more deeply and delve into some of the steps that you can take to bring more authenticity to your life and your workplace.

## PSYCHOLOGICALLY SAFE IS SOUND

Most importantly of all, if people are going to show up as their authentic selves at work, they must feel safe enough to speak up and have a voice. This looks very different from everyone singing the same corporate song. While it's important for us to know our goals as a group, it's equally vital for each individual to know that their opinion, their skill set, and their expertise is recognized as valuable. How does this concept make you feel? Perhaps a little nervous, as if there's no longer one person steering the ship? Well, if anything, the events of 2020 have forced us to let go of the idea that any one person has "all the answers" and that sometimes we can benefit from letting many people have their say.

This means getting rid of a "my way or the highway" approach and allowing people from all areas of the business to express themselves. Before you jump to point out the difficulties in actioning this, please know that having run my own business for almost twenty years, I understand very well the importance of consistency in leadership and communication. But my experience has also shown me that this must be balanced by allowing each individual to have their say about the way things are done. Yes, it's often easier and faster to shut down potential for discussion and dissent and to keep forging ahead with the same old narrative. But at what cost? Nobody wants to live under a dictatorship, but this is essentially what's happening in the workplace when we take this approach.

In my own workplace, where we regularly review reports from a quality perspective to ensure they are meeting requirements, I always encourage team leaders not to over-correct. Yes, we need to make sure each document is sound, but we don't want to drown out the writer's voice; we don't want everyone to sound the same. We want to encourage people to have their own style and way of conveying their message. It is too easy to say, "This is *the* way we do things here." What takes real skill, and what cultivates a culture of authenticity, is staying curious and remaining open to other people's ways of getting things done. This is how we allow our team members to have confidence in themselves and to develop their own voices in the world. They are learning a profession, yes, but they still get to be themselves.

Another advantage of taking this approach as a business is that it also leads to new ways of thinking. This lays the foundation for innovation and creativity, which in turn is what makes a good company *great*! The world is moving too fast for us not to be evolving and innovating as we go, and companies that do not adopt this attitude will be left behind in the dust. This sort of approach is more important now than ever. As we face challenges we have never come up against before, we will need to employ as many different minds and ideas as possible to find the solutions that will help our businesses to thrive. This is not the time to shut people down; let your people have a voice, and you will come out ahead.

Once you have identified this as a goal, it's not enough to simply ask people to speak up—there must be an active process of giving people permission to be themselves as they enter your doors. What do I mean by this? Most people will have come from families, schools, and other groups where they have been rewarded for fitting in—even if this means keeping parts of themselves shut down or hidden away. This conditioning runs deep and makes people fearful of speaking up, and so we often need to proactively encourage the opposite and rewrite this script in order to let people know that they will not be ostracized for being authentically themselves.

One way to start is with a "team values" exercise. This is easy to implement, and people are always surprised at what comes up, as well as how much it helps team members to understand one another and work together better. We so often presume we know what's driving people (what gives others' lives meaning), but these assumptions can get us into trouble. When we actively ask people to put their cards on the table, as it were, not only do we discover who we are really working with, but we also send a strong message that we want to get to know them and that we are interested in who they are.

Like anything, this exercise needs some planning to be effective. I provide the team with a list of values at least a week before the activity and ask them to choose the three that are most important to them. I also actively discourage people from separating these into "work values" or "home values," reminding them to approach the exercise as a whole person. I also suggest people take their time with this, maybe circling all the ones that ring true to them and then going back and narrowing the selection down to the three that feel most important to them over the following couple of days. I also ask people to consider how they feel they are living by these values and where they feel their values are challenged, and I ask them to come to the group with examples they are happy to share.

When team members feel comfortable, they can come back together to discuss with the group what their values are and how they feel they are living their values either in their work lives or their home lives. I did this exercise with many teams in 2020, and most people used it as a time to also reflect on their experience with the pandemic and how it had, in most instances, reminded them about the importance of living by their values. As I have said in the past, you might be skeptical about how willing people will be to participate in these types of activities, but I am confident that you will be pleasantly surprised by the candor that people bring to this exercise. I think this just shows how valuable bringing authenticity to your team can be.

When we did this exercise with my team, one of my colleague's values was "order." He shared that he was able to bring his best self to work when he knew that everything in his life had its place, allowing him to rise to whichever situation was presenting itself. Not only did this make sense; it also allowed me to understand him so much better, and I could see that questions he would ask that sometimes seemed pedantic were actually about him establishing the order that he so valued, making me more patient with him and cognizant of providing this level of structure for the team as a whole. Neuroscience tells us that when we name things, we are better able to manage them. By naming our values in this way, we are better able to manage and support our colleagues' needs—making it easier to get along and to work efficiently and effectively together.

The next step is even more important: once you have done the values exercise as a team, it's vital to keep the conversation alive. Again, this won't just happen; you have to make it happen. You might build a segment into staff meetings where people can talk about how they have lived their values in the last week or, alternatively, had their values challenged—both great prompts for an authentic conversation. So often we feel these opportunities to be candid and open are only for the yearly planning day or a one-off workshop. Taking this time regularly lets your team know it's a part of your day-to-day, and it becomes your company's culture, its story. If we have felt we had to put on a corporate coat to be accepted in the workplace, this is a testament to how liberating it is to be able to take that coat off and simply show up as ourselves.

Giving people space to speak their values provides a solid foundation for promoting authenticity at work. But we can take this a step further. For a workplace to be psychologically safe, people must feel confident about airing their opinions without fear of retribution. Many of us know the feeling of sitting in a meeting with an idea, something that we think might add value, but we don't speak up in case we'll be shot down—often because certain voices tend to drown out all the others or because we know our idea may upset the status quo. So how do we make it safe for everybody to have their say? One way is to include in your monthly meeting a space where each person gets to make a suggestion for something they'd like to change in the workplace. This puts "free speech" on the agenda and gives people time to prepare. This must also be backed up with action, so they also know that their suggestions will be taken seriously. Yes, this takes time and effort, but it also sends out the message that you are open to different ways of seeing things, and it will help people who usually feel that it's safer to stay silent to get more used to speaking up and bringing their ideas to the table. Like any other skill, sometimes this just takes practice.

Now I know there will be people reading this who absolutely don't feel that it is safe to be themselves at work and who also have no control over this. If this is you, please know that not every workplace is like this. Sometimes when we are in it, we think this is how the world works. Not true! If anything, in the aftermath of 2020, more and more people are realizing the value and importance of relating to one another as whole human beings. We are not robots, and we cannot continue to act or treat others this way. The workbook section below will help you think about what it might look like for you to bring more authenticity to your workplace. If this seems like it won't be possible in your current role, then at the very least it will show you what's not working in this area and why.

If you're a manager and you have the clout to bring more authenticity to your workplace but you're concerned that others may not be on board, you can congratulate yourself for at least considering what this might look like. Awareness comes first, and as with anything that's worthwhile, it takes effort to bring about changes to systems and ways of doing things that have become deeply entrenched over time. Engage with the work below to get an idea of what your goal is when it comes to creating a safe environment for people to be authentic, and consider what might be the first steps toward implementing this. Change doesn't have to happen overnight, but it will never happen unless you make a start.

## ❋ Workbook

1. Do you know your teams' values? The values exercise outlined above could get you started. You might like to try it with small teams first and then gradually introduce it to the broader workplace. How do you think you could start? If this feels outside your comfort zone, remember that doing things a little differently is often the start of change.

2. Once you know these values, how can you keep the conversation going at work? At our workplace we have a wall where we have all our values on display, as well as those of some of our regular clients. I can't tell you how many times I have stopped to look at that wall and found that it really helps me to understand something that's happening in our team. You could also establish a monthly or quarterly values exercise to track where you are.

3. How can you encourage people to have their say at your workplace? One team I work with has people give a two-minute summary of the highs and lows from their week at the beginning of their Friday meeting, with timed shares to give everybody their say. Even a small activity like this makes sure that everyone is regularly being heard and creates a space for the louder voices to step aside and make some room. What would work at your workplace?

## SICK OF THE BULLSH*T? ME TOO!

Most of the time, we just want people to level with us. We can all tell when someone is talking around something and avoiding the main message. Now, I am not advocating for running roughshod over people and bypassing being sensitive to others' opinions and needs. But when considering how you can let your team know you are keen for them to speak from the heart, it's important not to get lost in the land of jargon. While it's important to be respectful, being overly "PC" can also be a way of talking around issues that may be seen as "uncomfortable" or "unpleasant." But we're never going to make any progress if comfort is the primary goal. If we want to identify what is no longer working at work, we must be willing to have tough conversations—and if we can't name it, we can't change it.

When I was sixteen years old, I asked my brother to read an essay I had written; his advice was to not use big words when you can say the same thing using little ones, something I have never forgotten. As a manager, you can encourage the kind of plain speaking that lets people know what's actually going on while helping everybody feel included in leading by example and curbing your own use of the latest trendy language. What words will you drop first?

A great tool that Dr. Brené Brown uses is to begin a potentially confronting discourse with the following sentence starter: "The story I am telling myself is . . . ."[3] So often when trying to convey a difficult message, we go around in circles and do everything we can to avoid getting to the (uncomfortable) point. I think we've all been in conversations where we walk away shaking our heads, not really sure what was being said. People can smell a rat when this is the case, and while your intention might have been to avoid discomfort or conflict, all we ever really want to know is the truth. In addition, people will often come out of these interactions and then make up their own theories of what "might" be going on, which can lead everybody involved down a rabbit hole of conspiracies and confusion. By starting with "The story I am telling myself is . . . ," you automatically set the stage for an open-ended discussion, the implication being that your "version of events" is exactly that and acknowledging that there is likely more than one way to see things. By using this language, you are more likely to use plain speak as you outline your point of view, rather than tying yourself in knots trying to present a palatable "truth" that will not offend anybody. No pomp and ceremony is needed, and you do not need to "save face." In a culture of authenticity, you just need to let the other person know what's really going on.

As we have already explored, if you want to get clarity on how you are feeling or what you have to say, journaling is a great tool for self-reflection. It might also help you to identify where you are likely to "talk around" things and to discover what language you use when you are using your authentic voice. What sorts of words do you use when you freewrite and nobody is "watching"? How would your interaction shift if you used this kind of language in a conversation with a colleague that you have been putting off?

## ✳ *Workbook*

1. Is plain speak encouraged in your workplace? How would the company culture shift if people knew it was okay to be real with one another? Make some notes on how you think this impacts company culture and what changes you would like to see and why.

2. Which words are you going to ban from your vocabulary? Consider what kind of language makes you feel like you're being kept in the dark. Is this something you are guilty of too?

3. What situation in your life currently could you platform and address using "The story I am telling myself is . . ."? How would this change the way you speak about it with your team? What might the outcome be? You might like to practice with a friend first. Who would that person be? What makes it okay to tell it like it is with them?

## LISTENING 101:
## DO YOU HEAR WHAT I HEAR?

Do you know someone who's a really great listener? I do! Whenever I speak to her I get the feeling that she's really available and that she cares about what I have to say, and it makes such an enormous difference. We all need to feel heard. Knowing that our words have conveyed what we have to say, and that this has been received by somebody else, reinforces that we are valued. This not only bolsters our own sense of self but also reinforces our connection to the person who is listening. In an ideal world, we would carry out most of our conversations in a way that allows for this on both sides, but realistically this is not always the case. Even when we are trying our best, the pace of life and the sheer level of responsibilities we are juggling day-to-day means we are offering most people distracted listening.

When I work with organizations, I believe that the coaching I do on mindful listening is the one tool with potentially the greatest impact, especially given what I have identified as the three main problems when it comes to workplace well-being: the all-pervasive epidemics of mental health, loneliness, and tech addiction. As well as not feeling seen and heard in our increasingly individualistic lives, the beeps and pings and hypnotic nature of our devices make it hard for us to be fully available when someone talks to us. This makes learning the skill of active listening a potent antidote. So how do we regroup? How do we get this important skill back? As with anything, all it takes is practice.

A simple way to start is to create an exercise where team members pair up and each person gets to talk, uninterrupted, for five minutes. All their partner has to do is listen. No questions, no "that happened to me too," no giving advice; just listening. I love hearing people recount their experiences after this exercise; they often say things like "It was so hard not to ask questions," "I can't believe how much I remember about what they said," and "I think I understood them better." It is also important to note that as well-meaning as our questions and assurances might be, they often derail something important that the person talking needed to say, especially if it's something authentic and therefore vulnerable, as you interrupting gets them off the hook from sharing it. By leaving space in the conversation for them to simply talk, we give them the opportunity to get whatever it is "off their chest."

Following this exercise, I often ask the groups I work with to practice "stealth" mindful listening—they pick a day when they really focus on listening, without telling anybody this is their intention. This means being really conscious of not interrupting people and focusing on what a person is saying as opposed to sitting there and thinking about what you want to say next (something I know we're all guilty of, especially when we feel like we need to "impress" them or appear like we have it all together). Again, the feedback following this exercise is amazing; people are blown away by how much more they feel heard, not just in their interactions with work colleagues but also, perhaps even more importantly, with their families and friends.

This also works both ways. In the majority of relationships, we often get stuck in the role of being either the talker or the listener, and practicing active listening can also shine a light on where we could perhaps benefit from speaking up as we begin to notice how we allow others to take up all the talking space. This can be very uncomfortable if you're used to staying quiet—perhaps you notice that your taking pride in being a "good listener" is also a way to keep your needs and opinions to yourself, as it feels "risky" to speak up. But we need to hear from you too.

## ❋ Workbook

1. I love seeing people's reactions to mindful listening more than any other practice. Try the practice I have outlined above with your team; it only takes about twenty minutes. The most important part of the exercise is taking time to reflect afterward, so make sure you take the time to really encourage people to explore what they might have heard differently following this exercise.

2. We often get into habits with our family and friends around listening. What role do you play with different

individuals in your life, and why? If you usually do most of the talking, how might your relationships shift if you held back on the commentary? How might your questions differ if you were really focused on learning what's going on for the people in your life?

3. Take a day to practice "stealth listening." At the end of the day, note how this impacted the quality of your interactions. What did you learn about the people in your life? What do you remember about what they said, and how did it feel to see them in a different way?

## ARE YOU GOING IN THE RIGHT DIRECTION?

In order to be authentic, we also need to have some confidence in the direction we are headed and the decisions we are making. We've all had times when we've known deep down that the road that we're headed down is perhaps not the best, but for whatever reason we have continued in the same direction. We have avoided listening to that niggling voice in our head that tells us something is off. But this voice will find a way to get our attention—as the poem "Autobiography in Five Chapters" by Portia Nelson illustrates:

**Chapter One**
I walk down the street.
There is a deep hole in the sidewalk.
I fall in.
I am lost . . . I am helpless.
It isn't my fault.
It takes forever to find a way out.

### Chapter Two
I walk down the same street.
>There is a deep hole in the sidewalk.
>I pretend I don't see it.
>I fall in again.
I can't believe I am in this same place.
>>But, it isn't my fault.
It still takes a long time to get out.

### Chapter Three
I walk down the same street.
>There is a deep hole in the sidewalk.
>I see it is there.
>I still fall in . . . it's a habit . . . but,
>>my eyes are open.
>>I know where I am.
It is *my* fault.
I get out immediately.

### Chapter Four
I walk down the same street.
>There is a deep hole in the sidewalk.
>I walk around it.

### Chapter Five
I walk down another street.[4]

What I like the most about this poem is how gentle it is. Nelson does not berate us for repeatedly making the same mistake; she simply recognizes that even when things do not end well for us, it can be challenging to change our ways. That often it takes time and many lessons until, ultimately, we are in a position to make another choice. There is no need for guilt or for blame, simply awareness. This presents an opportunity for self-reflection about the things we could do differently. When we can gently assess and course correct, until we feel good about the street we are traveling down, our confidence in ourselves and our choices builds. Over time, we feel more connected to who we are, more authentic.

In contrast, I often see a cycle play out whereby an individual or an organization feels a "mistake" has been made, and they immediately become highly critical and even abusive toward themselves and members of the team. The fight-or-flight response of the amygdala is activated, and along comes the adrenaline that accompanies this type of reaction. In addition to laying on the shame and making it harder for people to speak up with possible solutions, it's harder to make sound decisions from this space. Before we know it, a simple human error has had a lasting negative impact.

If instead we can find the tools to recognize when something has gone wrong, finding ways to express our frustration and disappointment without going into attack mode, then we won't spiral into this adrenaline fugue. This begins with accepting that we are, indeed, only human, and that mistakes will always happen. From this starting place, we have a much better chance of being able to respond as a team, using all of our higher problem-solving skills. Can you feel how this will inevitably result in a far better outcome? Not to mention leaving us with more energy in the tank to course correct and get back on track.

We don't tend to have much time for gentleness and compassion in our highly competitive workplaces, and when I talk about these concepts with my clients it can lead to some eye-rolling. But while it can seem woo-woo or a little bit warm and fuzzy for places where the focus is usually on the bottom line, it also makes good business sense. When you look at the neuroscience of decision-making, we know this is compromised when the amygdala is running the show and when we are reacting to a perceived threat versus responding in a creative and innovative way. So, if you want a business with critical thinkers who are able to grapple with complex problems without wasting time on blaming and shaming, then it is vital to create a culture where it's okay to make mistakes in the name of progress.

So often we feel our mistakes are something that must remain hidden, but it is hard to be authentic if these are constantly kept out view. They are part of the human experience, and, dare I say it, I think most of us know this is where we learn the most about ourselves and figure things out. So, if we know authenticity is good for us and good for our teams, that means owning our mistakes and managing them in a gentle way that does not send us into a spiral of blame, guilt, and shame.

## ❋ *Workbook*

1. Think of a time recently when things didn't go so well. Write down what happened, including how you and your team responded: Was it a fight-or-flight scenario? Taking into account the above, make some notes about what you might have done differently. If you "reacted" (perhaps out of fear of losing face) what could you have done to "respond" instead?

2. Are there other areas of your life where you feel that it is time to course correct? This might be just a "niggly" voice in your head, or it might be a problem or an interaction with someone else that appears to be playing on repeat in your life. Other signs that people often discuss with me are not sleeping, being snappy at home, replaying conversations from work at home, or feeling that they are not able to wind down without a few glasses of wine.

Sometimes just sitting quietly allows you to hear a little more clearly. How can you carve out a little more time to hear this voice?

---

## IT'S GOOD TO BE KIND

Another important factor to consider when we think about being authentic is kindness. Yep, I'm sure we can all agree that we need more kindness in the world! But beyond being kinder and less judgmental toward others, and in doing so letting them know that it's safe to be themselves, what I actually want to talk about here is kindness to self, or self-compassion. To be authentic, we need to have a level of acceptance of where we're at, right now. To be able to look in the mirror each morning and acknowledge, "This is who I am, and that's okay." We may not always see the person who we hoped to be or who has achieved all the things we thought we would have by this age, but it's important to recognize that we are always doing the very best we can with the resources that are available to us.

How does this feel? We live in a world that paints a "picture-perfect" image of what it means to be a successful human being and which in turn does not encourage this level of acceptance and kindness toward the self. So on the mask goes, while underneath we undermine ourselves for not "looking" as good as everyone else. But being authentic, and meeting yourself where you're at, means no more bashing yourself for what you see as your failures and shortcomings. Imagine if you gave yourself the same permission to be working it out as you go along as you would a close friend or loved one.

One way to start being kinder to your authentic self is to take note of your self-talk. Using your active listening skills, anytime you find yourself criticizing yourself, jot down some of the things you say. Would you speak to anyone else in your life like this? Probably not unless you wanted to belittle them so that they never felt it was okay to speak up. So why is it okay to speak this way to ourselves?

Ultimately, you are the person with whom you have the closest, most intimate relationship of all. It's very hard to feel good about ourselves and how we show up in the world when the inner voice is so loud and so harsh. Dr. Kristin Neff, the cofounder of the Center for Mindful Self-Compassion, outlines some easy practices in her work to reframe our self-talk—such as writing a letter to yourself as if you were talking to a friend who was struggling with the same concern as you, or simply noting three to five things that you appreciate about yourself daily.

By bringing acceptance and kindness to all the different parts of ourselves, we begin to repair the schism between the people we think we should be and the people we are today—until there is just one authentic person showing up for all the different roles we play. Soon we'll feel confident enough to always say, "Here I am, all of me!"

## ✳ *Workbook*

1. For the next couple of days, try to become aware of how you are talking to yourself. When something happens, good or bad, simply notice what you are telling yourself about it and make a note of this. Go back and have a look at these notes a few days later. Most of us are harder on ourselves than we think, and gaining some awareness of this is the first step toward making a change.

2. Having become aware of our language, the next step is to try to catch ourselves and reframe it. For example, if

you find yourself calling yourself an "idiot," you might instead say something like, "You know you did the best you could." As with any ingrained behaviors, this isn't going to change overnight. But with practice you'll be surprised how quickly you start treating yourself with a little more kindness.

3. How could you be kinder to yourself this week? I often talk to people who are going through a tough time at work, be it the workload or the nature of the work. I suggest they do something special for themselves on the weekend. In a lot of cases, it seems like such a foreign concept, and these clients literally don't know what that would look like. I am not sure what it is for you, but for me I always love being in a bookshop, so carving out the time to visit one is a real treat. For some clients, it might be having a massage or going for a high tea or even something as simple as lying in the bath. I am just suggesting that you are proactive, when things are tough, about making sure there is something in your life that will bring you a little spark of joy. What could you do for yourself that is a little kind and a little gentle this week?

---

Working on our authenticity as individuals and as a group supports connection. It is impossible to connect to something that is not real. Encouraging our people to develop the skills that support an authentic workforce enables our parts and the sum of our parts to become a whole, and we know this makes us greater. In chapter 5 we are going to explore how to embed all the important practices we are learning into our everyday so that they become part of the DNA of our organization.

# CHAPTER 5

# GROUND RULES

A workplace that understands the value of meaning, and which allows its people to express themselves with authenticity, is well on the way to becoming an environment where everybody can thrive. The next piece of the puzzle is to establish a set of ground rules so that people don't need to "sweat the small stuff." They know how things run and they know what to expect. My experience is that when people have this type of stability in their organization, it frees them up to get the job done.

Ground rules are the key to steadying a rudderless ship and to feeling stable in a world with so many unknowns. For this reason, determining which ground rules are appropriate for your workplace begins with knowing, first and foremost, what we need to feel solid at work—meaning the things we need in place so we can relax, take a deep breath, and get on with the work at hand without constantly worrying if we're about to be steered off course. Without ground rules, burnout is inevitable, as all our energy is consumed trying to guess what comes next. But the magic lies in establishing a set of rules that are flexible enough to take everybody's needs into account while allowing space for the innovation that will help an organization adapt and evolve with the times.

Ground rules are particularly valuable when it comes to communication and conflict in organizations. Think of them as providing a detailed map that will get you safely from A to B. Note here I did not mention that this would necessarily be a comfortable, swift, or particularly easy trip; to engage with one another in an authentic and healthy way takes commitment, focus, and energy, and you might find yourself exhausted by the time you reach your metaphorical destination. Rather, the desired outcome is for all involved to remain connected to one another and to the values and goals of the team.

Most organizations I work with don't have any official guidelines in place about how to deal with difficult communication, decision-making, or conflict. This is puzzling, given that these are a given when you bring groups of people together. And herein lies part of the problem. Despite evidence to the contrary, we tend to operate under the myth that we humans are supposed to get along all of the time (similar to the myth that every family is a happy one) and that by engaging in conflict we are somehow betraying this hidden code. This can lead to fear and judgment about not being a good "team player" or bringing bad vibes to an organization or project. But the truth is, we are never all going to see things the same way—and this is a *good* thing, remember? If we want innovation and creativity, we need to hear from multiple points of view. Which is where a set of robust ground rules outlining how we manage these "tricky" situations comes in. Let's dive in a little deeper.

## THIS IS WHO WE ARE,
## AND THIS IS HOW WE WORK

So where to begin when establishing your ground rules? So much of this comes down to the people who make up your workforce—what gives them meaning and what being authentic means to them. As a workplace mediator, the variety in different backgrounds between workers sometimes astonishes me. Considering our various family lives, educations, religious backgrounds, and political views, it's amazing that we are all able to get along. These differing backgrounds also mean we come to a workplace with assumptions about how things will (and should) be done. Essentially, we view our working lives through the lens of where we have come from and what we believe is the right way of doing things.

In mediation sessions, we often work on unpicking and averting some of these assumptions. We might explore what "professional" means for one person or what "respect" means for another. How would you demonstrate these qualities? What examples would you give for how this should look at work? You'd be amazed at the differences in how people interpret words we use every day in our workplaces, while taking it for granted that we're all reading from the same page. Too often, differences in opinion about what constitutes "respectful" behavior, for example, leads to conflict and a breakdown in communication, which is when I get called in. But establishing your company's ground rules goes a long way when it comes to preventing this from happening in the first place.

This begins with spelling out what our assumptions are as individuals, which will often involve determining what constitutes meaning and authenticity for people and then deciding as a group what will work for everyone. In my experience, this process alone could provide the manual for "Making Work Work Again!"

One way to start to understand the assumptions people are working under is to get everyone together and choose three to four topics you feel are relevant to how you work as a team and then have everyone give their view on what this means to them or how this should work. You might begin with some modes of conduct we associate with work but which mean different things to different people; "respect" and "professionalism" are two good examples. Canvas the group and write everybody's interpretation of these words up on a white board, and from there drill down what a *shared* interpretation or set of values for each word might be for your group. Keep culling, until you get to just three key points that people can keep front of mind when they are considering their actions at work.

Alternatively, you might choose to explore ground rules around the ways you operate as an organization. For example, what does a good meeting look like, where do we go wrong with emails, and how do we make decisions? An important part of this exercise is to genuinely explore everyone's experiences so people can get insight into how and why others might see things differently. Once you have heard everybody's point of view, consider what is going to work for you as a team. Not only will you have a clear action plan in each of these different areas and a road map for "this is how we do things here"; this exercise is also guaranteed to help bring you together as a team and to ensure that people don't just feel as if they're being dictated to from the top. When everybody is brought in from the beginning, it fosters a culture of ownership and account-ability when it comes to adhering to your ground rules.

Looking at people's assumptions about what's import-ant and how they *think* things should be done will help you get clarity on the ground rules you need in place to ensure that your people feel seen, safe, and secure in their roles at work. As you begin to formulate yours, I have outlined some of the ground rules from my own organization and the companies I work with below:

- We speak *to* people, not about them.
- Running late for meetings says I think my time is more important than others'.
- Conflict is okay.
- Authentic communication is our way.
- We are curious.
- Clear is kind.
- We like to listen.
- We are grateful.
- We do not gossip.

Do any of these resonate with you? Or perhaps do they not necessarily feel like a fit for your workplace? Use the exercises in the workbook section below to get into the nitty-gritty of what will work for your people.

## ✳ *Workbook*

1. To kick off, I suggest you try the exercise I outlined above. Pick the activities or areas of conduct that feel like they are the most important for your team to explore. For example, you might have noticed that meetings aren't flowing well, or that things are getting lost in communication over email. It's important to take time to explore everybody's understanding of these different areas, so do not rush this stage. You could approach this exercise in two parts: first get everybody's ideas down, and then get them to go away and think about what is most important

to them. You can then reconvene and have a vote about the ground rules you want to adopt as a group. At my workplace we drilled into our values using this exercise. By considering what "integrity" meant to us as a group, we got to the following:

- Do the right thing.
- Be clear.
- Do what you say you are going to do.

When it came to health and well-being at work, we landed on:

- Water your own garden first.
- It is okay to ask for help.
- Have fun.

Think about this exercise as like pulling at a thread to untangle a knot. The more questions you ask and the more you explore, the more clarity you will uncover about who you are as individuals and what you might need as a team.

2. Once you have clarity around people's assumptions, you can start working on which ground rules you want to put in place. Some of the key areas to start with when considering ground rules are:

- **Communication**—what does good communication look like?
- **Conflict**—what do we do when we butt heads?
- **Decision-making**—how do we make decisions?
- **Meetings**—what works and what does not?

Rather than trying to tackle everything at once, pick one topic at a time and delve deep. As we did above, get everyone's ideas down about what ground rules will work for your organization and then have a vote on the three your team thinks are most important. If you're finding it difficult to get down to three, maybe review what came up for you in the chapter on meaning; this might help you see which ones are most aligned with where you want to get to.

3.  Once you have established your ground rules, you need to make them front and center of your organization. This means embedding them in your recruitment and induction process. At recruitment, you might also ask the candidate what they feel are their ground rules for successful meetings, for example. You'll be surprised at how this can shine a light on whether they are a good fit to join your team and become part of the culture that you have been working hard to build. When it comes to reminding existing team members of your ground rules, you could make a video or a podcast that outlines what they are and how you came to these as a group. Take some time now to think about how you can introduce your ground rules to your existing teams and how to embed them in the recruitment and induction processes.

4.  Ground rules can be especially helpful when it comes to getting back on track when things have gone wrong at work. As an exercise for reflection, think about a time when things weren't going well, and see if you can identify a ground rule that was obviously missing in the situation. For example, if one of your ground rules is "we do what we say we are going to do," you will be able to start a conversation about why this didn't happen from a neutral

place, rather than it feeling like any one individual is pointing the finger and assigning blame.

5. As a last exercise before we move on, put aside time for a regular review of your ground rules. The world and the ways in which we work are changing at a rapid pace, and this means our ground rules need to evolve as we do. This might become part of your annual review, or it could be something you do seasonally or when you land a big new contract. Whatever you decide, make sure that you have a clear idea of when your ground rules will be reviewed. We don't want them to end up as tired old tropes that have lost all their meaning for people. Instead, think of them as the glue that keeps you together; this is how we make work work for us!

Now that you've considered the kinds of ground rules your people need the most, let's look at some areas where you can get more specific.

## THE ART OF COMMUNICATION

A lot of my work involves sitting in on workplace mediations. I always meet with both parties prior to a mediation, and generally there is a lengthy discussion on what went wrong. Often, it is the speed at which we lead our lives that leads to crossed wires, together with our assumptions about what people mean that we have set into stone in our own minds before actually exploring (being curious) about whether we actually *do* understand where the other person is coming from. But when we get to the mediation day and I have two people sitting across from each other, looking each other in the eyes, I often find things play out very differently.

Simply put, this is because when we create space to talk things out in person, we are able to have more compassion for one another as human beings. We might remember that our "adversary" also has a sick parent at home or a teenager who's going through a tough time. Now we're not quite as willing to "let them have it." Most importantly, setting up an official mediation session lets people know they will have a space to be fully seen and heard, and this is pure gold when it comes to successful communication in general.

So often, miscommunication occurs when we are rushing through life. This is when assumptions can become "shortcuts" to understanding; too busy to double-check, we assume our first impression of a situation must have been correct, and we proceed with a skewed view of what has transpired. Or in another "time-saving" effort, we rush off an email rather than pick up the phone to explain what's going on—especially tempting when we know deep down that the matter we are discussing is contentious and that we might meet with resistance from the other person. In both these scenarios, we assume (again) that it's best to get things done as quickly and with as little "fuss" as possible. But what if instead your ground rules around communication were:

- If you are questioning how an email will be received, don't send it; pick up the phone and talk to the person instead.
- If you come away from a conversation feeling unclear (or, as I describe it, feeling a little "fuzzy"), go back and ask some questions.

These are just suggestions, and you might choose completely different ground rules for your team. But when it comes to communication, considering rules that address the adrenaline-fueled way we speed through life can be helpful. What would encourage curiosity and, dare I say it, a little kindness in your communication? These simple interventions could help avoid the kind of needless conflict that ultimately prevents work from getting done but also impacts the health and well-being of both individuals and teams.

Here are some things to get clear about as we begin:

### What does good communication look like?

Each workplace is different, but this means getting clarity about what is a "yes" and what is a "hell no" when it comes to communication in its many forms.

A good first step is to consider when to use which methods of communication—when is it okay to send an email, and when is it essential that you pick up the phone, arrange a videoconference, or actually meet face-to-face. Let's not forget that an estimated 93 percent of our communication is nonverbal, meaning important cues get lost in an email. Talking things out face-to-face also makes it easier to go back and forth to clarify parts of the message; again, this is not so easy in an email exchange. One of my clients told me she can now tell when she is typing with "angry fingers" and that that is her sign to delete that draft and to get clear on why she is feeling so triggered before setting up a time to talk to the person instead.

Getting this simple step right can make an enormous difference. People rarely come into a workplace mediation without a trail of emails that have gone wrong. If only at some stage someone had picked up the phone or, where possible, arranged a coffee to talk things out, the situation might never have escalated to the point where a mediator needed to be called in. Why is this so important? No one skips into a mediation, and by the time people get to me, the situation has likely impacted not only their work but their home life too. They're not sleeping, they may feel physically unwell, they may have been drinking more, and they have been snapping at their family and friends. Anything we can do to prevent things going this far is time well spent.

## How do we manage conflict?

Following on from the themes above, I think a great ground rule is to lay out how you manage conflict during induction. Yes, you heard me right. This might not feel like the friendliest way to introduce people to your organization, but when people are clear on this from day one, it shows that you recognize the reality that sometimes people don't get along—and that that's okay. You're also saying that you are committed to supporting people in finding solutions in a manner that demonstrates respect and keeps all involved safe.

In my experience, more often than not an organization's approach to conflict is to dig a very big hole and to put their head in it. But this only worsens the situation, for both the individual parties involved and those who work alongside them, and if you're committed to a workplace that puts psychological safety front and center, this is something you need to address. To begin to rethink attitudes toward conflict in your workplace, you might let people know that it's natural for us not to get along all the time—especially in an environment where people are encouraged to have their own opinions, as sometimes these are bound to rub against one another. This means having some ground rules in place to ensure that we explore options and consider different points of view and that we do this with people's psychological safety front of mind.

Examples of ground rules to address the above two points might be:

- We don't allow things to fester. When we can see there is a problem, we lean in to any discomfort and make sure people come together to discuss it, as opposed to the head-in-the-sand approach favored by many workplaces.
- We have people in our workplace who have specialist skills in negotiation or facilitation, and we have external resources that we can call on if required. The most important thing is that this is discussed honestly and plainly and seen as just part of business and not some dirty secret.

Another great ground rule appeared up above: "We speak *to* people, not about them." A mentor of mine, Di McDonald, implemented this ground rule as follows; she called it Penny/Jane/Bill. If Penny has a problem with Bill, the person she needs to speak to is Bill. What often happens instead, however, is that, fearing conflict, Penny will speak to Jane instead of raising her issue directly with Bill. But when Penny speaks to Jane, nothing changes. All she has really done is spread "bad feeling" about Bill, creating toxicity along the way, something I see playing out in workplaces every day.

By introducing the Penny/Jane/Bill "rule" at induction, as we did in our organization, not only are you encouraging clear communication between individuals, but you are also giving people permission to speak up when approached with a gripe about somebody else. You can simply say, "Sorry, Penny/Jane/Bill," which is code for "We don't gossip here; it's not helpful."

This is a great practice among colleagues, but it will also work for a manager who finds herself listening to a team member who wants to unload about a colleague without actually doing anything to challenge their behavior. Without a doubt, it takes courage to speak to people face-to-face. But once it's established as a collective practice, it makes it less about "conflict" and more about simply keeping us all on the same page and getting the job done.

When can you explore some of these themes with your team? As we've established, this means canvassing differing attitudes and assumptions among your workforces, a process that takes time and conscious effort, but it will save you so much in the long run. When people have clarity in these areas, they won't be wasting time worrying about mixed signals, trying to decipher what someone might have meant, or trying to second-guess how a situation will play out. This frees up time and energy to be applied to the work at hand, along with the brainpower needed for creativity and innovation. It's estimated that 50 percent of a manager's time is spent managing conflict;[1] can you imagine if you had all that time to apply to creative problem-solving instead?

## ❊ *Workbook*

1. To begin, consider what ground rules you already have in place around communication and conflict. Notice how many of these are "unspoken" (and therefore "assumptions" of your own). Write them down.

2. Now begin to map out what ground rules could be helpful in these specific areas. There are so many ways you could go with this, and it's okay to start small and not try to find all the answers overnight. Perhaps you can begin with what is okay and not okay when it comes to email. Set aside an hour to get your team together to explore this. I promise you that getting some consistency around this practice alone will make an enormous difference.

3. The next thing to explore as a team is what you might do if you feel like the temperature is starting to rise in an interaction. Nobody I have ever worked with doesn't understand what I mean by this. Your ground rules in this instance might be to actually state out loud what's happening: "I don't think we are seeing eye to eye. Is there another way we can be looking at this?" It might be to ensure that once you recognize there is friction, you are banned from email communication on the matter and may only discuss it on the phone or face-to-face. Or perhaps it's that you have a third party available to facilitate some broader problem-solving. These are just a few suggestions, and I think you will be pleasantly surprised by how keen your team will be to talk about their experiences previously, noting what worked and what absolutely did not. Again, set aside an hour with your team and just tease out this specific question. Remember to let people know that this is about helping people feel safe to be themselves at work.

4. Once again, it is important to embed these in your induction process. You might make a podcast or a YouTube clip where different people discuss the ground rules of your organization and how you came up with them. This will ensure that from the minute a new employee steps foot in your organization, they know what to expect and they won't be tempted to bring the practices of their previous workplace with them.

## MEETING ONE ANOTHER WHERE WE ARE

Once you have committed to some of your ground rules around communication and conflict, you can spend some time exploring your rules around how you meet and commune more broadly as an organization. I think most of us could probably write a whole book on all the ways that meetings can go wrong, which is such a shame when you think of the opportunities that *can* open up when we come together as a group. Getting all your "people power" in one place should be when the magic happens. But how many of us see meetings in this light? More often than not, they are seen as an opportunity for a little snooze, with people making an intermittent yes or no to give others the impression they are actually in the room. But with a few simple ground rules around this part of our working lives, meetings can be used to harness the power of the collective.

Where to begin? Meetings go wrong when individuals' needs are not addressed. For example, in the last chapter, I mentioned that one of my colleagues' top two values is "order"—so a workplace where everyday practices, including meetings, are haphazard will negatively impact his overall well-being and productivity. I guarantee there will be people on your team like him, but even for those that can handle a little more fluidity, not having to worry about the small things will take a mental load off.

Consider your answers to the following questions:

- When do we meet?
- How do we set up a meeting?
- Who determines the agenda?
- Do we even have an agenda?
- Is there space to add to the agenda?
- Do we take minutes?

- Who writes these minutes?
- Is it all business, or is there room to get to know the people behind the titles?
- Do we have a mindfulness or gratitude practice as part of our meeting?

If you cannot answer these questions easily, then you have some work to do. It might seem pedantic to have specific ground rules for meetings, but take a moment to consider how many times you've found yourself annoyed by small things just like these while in a meeting. Our brains crave certainty, and getting clarity around how we interact and commune as an organization and as a team means less time figuring this out. Again, this allows us to use this brain space elsewhere: actually doing our work, focusing on solutions, and being creative.

## ❋ Workbook

1. Reflect on which daily practices feel like they are already set in stone in your workplace. Jot these down. Once you have completed this list, the next step is to consider where the gaps might be. What do you think is missing? Jot these down as well.

2. In the list of gaps, which three are a priority for you to address? How might getting more clarity in these areas make a difference for your team? If you need help with this, find time to discuss what annoys people the most. I'm sure they will be happy to tell you!

3. Now repeat the exercises from above about establishing ground rules in these areas that feel like a priority for the people who make up your team.

## HOW DO WE GET THINGS DONE?

Research tells us that we are distracted from the task at hand 47 percent of the time.[2] In our working lives, this obviously has a huge impact on our overall productivity. With this in mind, let's make sure that you also have some ground rules around how you focus and get things done. In a world where the tech epidemic makes focus increasingly hard to achieve, this means considering how we can establish routines that support focus and concentration. It makes sense that this should be something that organizations inherently recognize as a positive, but, more and more, "busyness" has become the badge of honor—and "busyness" does not necessarily equate to getting the job done.

This process begins with creating ground rules around tools to bring us back into the present moment—which sounds simple but which is trickier in practice. Why is this so important? Psychologist Rick Hanson's work points to the "negativity bias" of our brains, whereby our minds are like Velcro for negative thoughts and Teflon for positive ones. This means that when we're distracted at work, we're usually not thinking about that holiday we had in Fiji or our plans for the coming weekend; we're more likely ruminating on something that's gone wrong in the past or something we have coming up that we anticipate will be challenging. Sitting at our desks, in the here and now, we are perfectly safe and sound—but with our minds elsewhere, the negativity bias often causes a stress response in the body. Therefore, having tools available that bring you into the present moment allows you to remain in the safe space of the here and now, where you are simply more available to put your energy into the job in hand.

This means that the emphasis is on focus—and the importance of having ground rules to support this—is two-fold. Sure, focus supports concentration, leading to greater productivity, but it also helps to combat the negativity bias, which in turn supports our overall psychological health and well-being.

When considering how to establish ground rules in this area, the first step is to explore the mindfulness tools that are already available so you can find the right fit for you and your team. Before you introduce these ideas—which often fall outside of the usual remit of workplace protocols—it's also important to make sure people understand why they are doing this. Then it's time to explore how you can include these practices in your working day. These tools will help you to regain focus anytime you notice that your mind has wandered, will aid you in regrouping after a difficult conversation or email, and will help you to recenter anytime you feel the adrenaline starting to pump throughout the day. Again, providing education around this during induction will lay the groundwork for you.

You may begin with something small—for example, a ground rule that says you begin each meeting with just one minute of mindfulness. Explain that this will allow people to leave behind what they were doing and arrive fully in the room. This might mean having them breathe into their bellies or taking a minute to focus on the things around them that they can hear, see, feel, or smell. You may ask people to come back into their bodies by feeling their feet on the floor, feeling their bottoms on their chairs, and noticing the positions of their heads. Or you could use this time to set an intention for the meeting, such as "We will practice active listening" or "We will stay open and curious" or "We want everybody to get something positive out of this meeting." Now you have a room full of people who are focused, attentive, and available. It probably goes without saying, but another ground rule to support this might be having people leave their phones in a box by the door.

Sometimes, this is simply about remembering to do the things we already know are good for us. This is a bit like moving regularly and drinking enough water: we know we need to do it; we just need to remember to do it! Similarly, engaging in a regular mindfulness practice as a team reminds people how important it is to stay rooted in the present. If you're concerned you may get pushback around this subject, consider the workshop I did with one fellow who was really adamant that mindfulness was not for him. He went bushwalking every weekend, he told us, and that really cleared his head. But wasn't he surprised to find out this *was* a form of mindfulness? We went on to discuss what he could do to transfer some of the benefits of those weekend walks to the workplace as a team.

## ✳ Workbook

1. To begin educating your team about mindfulness, either suggest or organize a toolbox talk on the benefits of mindfulness in the workplace. You might use the many available resources online, or perhaps you could have an expert in to talk people through the benefits of these practices. The latter option will also give people the opportunity to ask plenty of questions.

2. Once you're aware of the options, choose one mindfulness practice that you can do as a team. I've mentioned a few throughout this book so far, and, as with most things, my advice is to start small. Every organization I have worked with has seen the benefits of, and has chosen to expand, their mindfulness program over time.

3. In addition, choose a specific practice to begin your meetings—even if these are happening over Zoom. Most

of us run into meetings or hop from one Zoom room to another so quickly we arrive feeling like our heads are spinning. Simply taking one minute for people to take some deep breaths, feel into their bodies, or even listen to a song or a positive affirmation—anything to bring people back into the here and now—will make a difference. Perhaps you can have a roster and somebody responsible for the practice for each meeting.

4. Even if you don't work on a team, consider what you can do as an individual so you are more present and really available for your meetings with clients. It might be that you pause other tasks and have a cup of tea prior to a meeting, taking a moment to feel the warmth and taste what you are drinking, or you might take one minute to look out the window and notice a tree outside, follow its branches, and notice all the different colors. It could be as simple as taking a big belly breath and slowly counting to five as you exhale before you hit "join" on Zoom. What do you think would work for you?

---

## WE ARE GRATEFUL: CELEBRATING YOUR WINS

And how about some ground rules around the good stuff? The pace of many workplaces means that as soon as one goal has been reached, we're often on to the next project without taking time to pat ourselves on the back for a job well done. But by taking an active pause to mark these moments, we build a tally of our achievements, and over time this helps us recognize our contribution and find more meaning in our work.

Meanwhile, having gratitude for the work we do helps

with the negativity bias discussed above. Given that we are naturally inclined toward the negative, balancing this with a regular practice that reminds us of what's going right can only be a good thing. And although it might seem counterintuitive, this means giving thanks for the challenges as much as for each new client or project that comes in. For example, I once explained to my daughter that a great consultant was leaving my company but that I was choosing to see this simply as one door closing while waiting for another door to open. In all of her nine-year-old wisdom, she said to me, "You know, Mum, I don't see it like that at all; I just see a long hallway with lots of doors opening all the time." When did we lose sight of that long hallway? When we have an active gratitude practice, I think we have a better chance of seeing endings or "failures" as opportunities too.

This is especially relevant in modern workplaces, where we often hear that change is the only constant. This can feel destabilizing, especially as we humans tend to resist change—even when it's change for the better. But taking time to appreciate and give thanks along the way can help us continue rising to meet whatever challenge might be around the next corner. Dr. Martin Seligman, the founding father of Positive Psychology, has said that "We think too much about what goes wrong and not enough about what goes right in our lives. . . . One way to keep this from happening is to get better at thinking about and savoring what went well."[3]

Is there space in your working life to savor "what went well"? As a manager, do you set aside time to celebrate the wins? Perhaps this means having a set time at a regular staff meeting for each person to reflect on a win; it could be an all-staff email when a compliment comes in; or maybe it's a wall of wins where you record things that go well on a big board in the office. It could just be a culture where "well done" and "good job" are part of the vernacular. What would work for you? Any of the above examples could become part of your ground rules.

We actually have lots of "rules" like these in our lives, but often rules about how we celebrate or reward ourselves remain unspoken: the piece of cake we allow ourselves after a project has been submitted; shutting off email at 5:00 p.m. on Fridays to kick off the weekend; switching our phone off on Sundays to give our nervous systems a break from being constantly on. Why not have specific workplace ground rules that speak to our achievements and our overall well-being as individuals too? We tend to think of rules as being about discipline, but we can subvert this by creating ground rules around having more fun! Rather than seeing them as limiting, what if our ground rules were always about giving ourselves more of what we need? When it comes to creating a set of workable ground rules for your workplace and your working practices as an individual, let's think about this as fostering an environment where new doors are always opening.

## ✳ *Workbook*

1. To begin to celebrate the positive, how about having a ground rule that you always end your meetings with a shout-out to anyone who's had a win? I often find that when this is embedded in the company culture as regular practice, people become more likely to send an email saying "well done" or to congratulate others vocally for a job well done.

2. If it doesn't feel like an option to bring this to your workplace right away, establish a ground rule around having a gratitude practice at home. Perhaps you take turns around the dinner table at night to share what went well

in your day. One client I worked with had a practice with his flatmates where they would message one another with one thing that was going well for them during the day. It's amazing how getting a text with some good news can lift your mood too.

3.  Another practice that's easy to implement is what I call the "wall of wins"—which means having a space in your office for people to share what's going well, both at work and in their personal lives. The beauty of this is that it's visible all the time, especially if it's positioned close to somewhere that people linger, such as by the kitchen or the photocopier. In the era of Zoom and working from home, you can create a space as part of your intranet page where people can share what's going well. You might then start meetings by reading out the most recent additions to your "virtual wall." And however it's displayed, your wall of wins also lets anyone visiting your organization know that celebrating one another is an important part of your culture—and that's a win right there!

More than ever, our lives are busy with so many competing demands. We need to make sure that we have ground rules in our workplaces to ensure that the practices that we know make work work are applied consistently. We can't just hope that we will be able to fit them into an already-overscheduled calendar. We need to clarify and prioritize what makes work work for our teams and embed this into our culture. With these ground rules in place, it's time to focus on the individual and how to celebrate the people that we work with every day.

# CHAPTER 6

## "I"

*If you are always trying to be normal, you will never know how amazing you can be.*[1]

**—MAYA ANGELOU**

**D**o you feel like you can be yourself at work, or is there an expectation that you don some kind of corporate mask before you enter the door? Does it feel like coming in just as yourself is categorically "not enough"? Alternatively, there might just be a complete indifference to the person you are on the inside at your workplace. Either way, this dynamic can make us feel like we are leading a double life. Part of who we are gets pushed aside during our working hours, and we exist as someone else entirely at the office or else are treated like a machine whose job is to simply deliver the product or service.

But the line between the work and home self has never been more blurred—to the point that there is virtually no longer any separation between the two. On the one hand, how things are going at work impacts the person we bring home. This works in our favor when we have a win at work;

we feel buoyed, and we walk away from our desks with a bounce in our step. But it equally works the other way; when things go south at the office, we can take our frustration out on those we love. Back in the mists of time, when you left your place of work for the day, you also left whatever was going on there behind. Some degree of separation was still possible, creating time and space for us to recover or at least recharge after a tough day. But thanks to the "gift of technology," we're expected to be available all the time, and there is much more seepage of our working life into our home life.

We now accept this simply as the way things are—but it typically only works in one direction: we bring our work home with us, and, to an extent, we're always on. But what if we balanced this by allowing the whole person that we are to come to work with us, rather than compartmentalizing our personalities and turning into corporate robots as we walk in the door? For those who feel they cannot be themselves at work, this may bring up feelings of either relief or trepidation.

Going back to the premise of MAGIC, we remember that when people do well at work, they do well at home, and vice versa. Doesn't it make sense, then, that when we see the two as interdependent, we can no longer keep our work selves and our home selves separate and expect either to flourish? Let's explore the concept a little more.

For example, why are we so often expected to leave the "I" at home? Too often, I see workplaces that have descended down a rabbit hole of productivity. Focused purely on the output, this extends to their people, who are often seen as automatons with piles of work to get done and key performance indicators that need to be accounted for. Corporate culture isn't entirely to blame for this—the overall pace at which we are living life, as referenced previously, does not lend itself to allowing people the space to be seen and heard or leave much time for the human behind the product or service to be acknowledged.

Ask yourself: Do you think your workplace sees the whole person who shows us up every day? Do they see the person who is courageously managing a chronic health condition, or the parent whose child is being bullied at school, or how the end of a relationship might have left a person feeling like their life has been upended? Or would this level of consideration for each individual's life outside the office be seen as an irrelevant distraction, only getting in the way of getting the work done? Perhaps there's part of you that's even thinking, *Who cares?*

Or maybe the opposite is true for you, and the higher-ups at your place of work go above and beyond to get to know the people on their teams. If this is the case, let's reflect on how this is done. Is it down to one or two people who are good at connecting on a more human level? Or is it something that's embedded in the ground rules of your workplace and demonstrated consistently throughout your organization?

I guess I'm asking whether welcoming all elements of each employee is part of the DNA of your workplace. If it is, you will be able to describe how it is woven into your recruitment process and through your induction program and then provide examples of how you see it playing out, day in and day out. The people you work with will be able to name it too, and they will be able to tell you how they are encouraged to get to know their colleagues or how they feel seen at work. If this is the case, your organization is onto something.

Our working world is now often referred to as VUCA— Volatile, Uncertain, Complex, and Ambiguous. If this is the reality of what we are walking into every day, then we are going to need both our heads and our hearts to make it through. In fact, we are going to need everything we've got! And this means bringing our whole selves to the office.

But what do I even mean by this "whole" self? Let's reconsider the values we have already explored in previous chapters as a prime example of the schism that often exists between our work selves and home selves. For example, when I do a values exercise with people, they always ask, "Are you talking about my work values or my values at home?" Inevitably people will identify their "home" values as things such as compassion and connection and their "work" values as things such as integrity and innovation. But how about we just have one set of values that we bring to everything we do? If we're willing to accept the premise that our work life can come home with us, then surely we can be open to the idea that our home values also have a place at work. But too often we feel we can only bring our heads to work, the "integrity and innovation" of our rational business minds, and that we must leave our hearts, which yearn for "compassion and connection," at home.

But in these times of almost constant change and uncertainty, problem-solving cannot only happen in our heads. We need to feel into the changes that are occurring, grieve the losses, and celebrate the opportunities with our hearts. For this reason, the "I" in MAGIC proposes bringing both our heads and our hearts to work. As we have seen, if you want your business to thrive, then this must begin with your people—which means making the time and space for them to be seen. We have explored the impact of the loneliness and mental health epidemics and their impact on workplace productivity and well-being. If you don't want your workplace to become a casualty of these epidemics, then it's time to quit worshiping at the church of "busyness" and take the time to really welcome the people walking through the door. Let's look further at how we can really see our people at work.

## I SEE YOU; I AM HERE

To foster real connection at work, the sort that will serve to keep people safe from the loneliness epidemic, people need to be able to show who they really are—and not feel they are just another cog in the wheel. Clocking in, day in and day out, without being able to share who you really are is a breeding ground for loneliness; you are somewhere, but you are not seen.

How do you "see" your colleagues at work? If this is an alien concept, what are the workplace practices that can be put in place to help us see one another? It might seem daunting, but as with most things, creating a culture where people feel seen begins with taking one or two small steps in a different direction. At the interview stage, it might mean asking a prospective employee how we would know if they were stressed—and, if we saw these signs, asking what would be the best thing we could do to support them. This might result in developing a self-care action plan, consisting of routines to support individual employees during difficult times. By putting this in place at the hiring stage, we are saying to the individual in question, "We want to see you—even when you're not perhaps at your 'shiniest.'" What a powerful message this would be to people starting with your organization.

It's also important to build some practices around connection into your everyday working lives. One that's easy to implement is promoting conversations that help you to get to know one another a little better. This may seem obvious, but how well do you really know the person you're sitting next to or Zoom conferencing with daily? This might be something you begin or end your regular team meeting with—which will also let people know that getting to know one another is most certainly "on the agenda." You might use a prompt to kick-start the conversation; for example, you might say: "What's something we don't know about you?" or "Tell us about a childhood memory." Or perhaps you might ask people to share about a trip that was special, in order to keep things a little lighter to begin with. You can also buy conversation-starter cards online, which have all sorts of different images on them to help prompt these types of conversations. The idea is that you pick a card and share whatever association comes up for you.

Alternatively, some of the teams I work with make time in team meetings to talk about a band they're into or share a movie or book they loved. The sky (or, rather, your imagination) is the limit in terms of when and how to implement these conversation starters, but with each one you'll get to know a little bit more about the person sitting next to you. This is how, over time, we learn that it's okay to bring the "I" to work and that being a valued employee is about so much more than how we deliver on a brief. Again, as I have mentioned before, this might feel "clunky" at first, but building these interactions into your ground rules will help foster a culture of "getting to know one another" in your organization over time.

## ❋ Workbook

1. What questions would you include in your recruitment process to let someone know you're keen to see the person behind the résumé? This could mean enquiries like:

   - How do you like to have fun?
   - What's a song that means something to you and why?
   - Who was your favorite teacher at school, and what was it about them that made such a difference?
   - Tell us about the teams you've worked in. Which was the best team, and what was your worst experience? What did you learn from both these experiences?

By stepping away from questions about the job and how it's done, you're giving them permission before they're even hired to bring their whole selves to your workplace.

2. What could you include in your induction that would signal to people that they're not just going to be treated like a number at your workplace? Getting people to explore their values and share them with the team is a good start. Another good step is creating the self-care plan mentioned above—beginning with making sure you are aware of what "stress" looks like for them and what things they have done in the past to support their well-being when the temperature begins to rise. When we know what to look for, it's sometimes easier to notice symptoms of stress from the outside than when we're the one in the thick of it. This could mean encouraging a culture where it's okay for workmates to gently ask, "Are you okay?" These are all signs of a workplace whose leaders are keen to see their people as people, not just corporate machines.

3. What conversation starters could you include in your meetings to help you all get to know one another a little better? It might seem that this won't make a difference, and for some it will seem a little twee. But if you hang in there and try it out, I think you'll be pleasantly surprised by some of the discussions that evolve, particularly when you get people talking about things like the music or places they love most—and why. When we delve into the why of these memories, it can uncover really important stories that help people better understand who we are.

## THE LONELINESS EPIDEMIC– LEANING IN, NOT LOOKING AWAY

The 2018 Australian Loneliness Report revealed that one in four Australians feel lonely each week. The same report also found that higher levels of loneliness are associated with higher levels of social-interaction anxiety, less social interaction, poorer psychological well-being, and poorer quality of life.[2] Meanwhile, the International Labour Organization estimates that around 61 percent of the world's working-age population participates in the labor market.[3] Given these statistics, it seems obvious that people's places of work—places where people are coming together regularly (even virtually)—provide an opportunity to address the loneliness epidemic head-on, a practice that could have an enormous impact on overall health and well-being.

Of course, your interests might not lie in contributing to the public health of the nation. But if you're reading this, then I'd hazard a guess that you are concerned with getting the best from your employees when they come to work. If this is your goal, then addressing loneliness by facilitating deeper connections at work will at the very least have a positive impact on the health of your people. And healthy people make up healthy teams, which in turn translates to a healthy bottom line.

In chapter 5, we explored the lost art of listening; certainly, being available to hear what people actually have to say is a great start when it comes to connecting with one another and making sure that people feel seen. But another important step is being able to be available to listen when someone needs *you* to share—or debrief—when something is not going well. This is more important than you might imagine. If we look into our history as a species, we know we have survived and thrived based on the strength of our group or tribe. So often in our current climate we feel we are flying solo, and this feeds into feelings of loneliness and depression. Rather than a culture of shame or blame, providing the people at your workplace with the skills necessary to support one another when something has gone pear-shaped, is an important step in combating feelings of isolation that ultimately diminish our potential as a team.

Do you feel that your workplace equips people with the skills to support their colleagues in this way? Providing training in this area further fosters the sort of connection we are talking about, as it helps people to feel safe about opening up when they're struggling or when something has gone wrong—a powerful antidote to the loneliness epidemic. When I provide this training, I'm always amazed at how engaged people are in learning this new skill. People want to be available, and they want to know how they can help, but often they feel out of their depth when it comes to providing this support.

So how do you skillfully ask somebody for an honest debrief?

My experience is that things often start off well. Somebody usually asks some questions to kick off the inquiry, and people tend to do well at explaining what happened and providing the facts. They capture the events and can outline quite objectively what went well—and where things went pear-shaped. People then tend to go straight to the action plan moving forward; once we've heard the details of what went wrong, we immediately want to figure out what we're going to do about it. This is very natural— broadly speaking, we don't like the "messy middle." We crave a degree of certainty, and we like to be able to tie things up with a neat little bow. But herein lies the problem. When we rush into action to "fix" something that's gone wrong, quickly slapping a Band-Aid over the problem, we are missing an important step, and our actions may leave the people involved feeling as if their experiences are not important to others.

So what could we do differently? Real "repair" means taking the time to stop and ask the person how they *feel* about what's gone wrong. In asking this question—and genuinely caring about the answer—we will get to a deeper understanding of what is happening for the person in front of us. But the bigger question might be: Do we really want to know the impact? Do we want to sit with and consider people's feelings, or is this a little inconvenient or uncomfortable? Feelings are messy, and sometimes we don't feel we have the space or the time to go there. When we ask in a genuine way, "How are you feeling?" we may not be ready for the answer. If the person in front of us replies that they feel incompetent, ashamed, guilty, angry, or embarrassed, what are we supposed to do with this information? You can be sure the action plan or strategies to address these feelings would be very different from any strategies put in place to fix whatever work issue has gone wrong.

For example, if somebody has had an incident where a customer has lashed out at them, they may feel all the emotions listed above. A manager may take stock of what has happened and leap straight into action mode, coming up with a script to be repeated by rote anytime an employee encounters a similar problem. But if instead they asked, "How did that make you feel?" they may find that the person is well-versed in how to handle "difficult conversations"—they just need another person to sit with them and hear how frightened or shocked they felt. They need somebody to recognize and validate their experience.

This type of exploration involves bringing both our heads and our hearts to work, and it often seems so much easier to rush to the next "solution" rather than sit with someone's emotions. But most work problems are *people* problems, and people have feelings. Skipping over this deeper line of enquiry is like trying to complete a one hundred–piece jigsaw puzzle when you only have ninety-three pieces.

Of course, we may feel we don't have the necessary skills to address the feelings that emerge—and this is absolutely okay. In fact, it's really important to recognize that this is the case. While some of us are naturally more versed in this area, it's not like we're all trained in psychology, and "emotional intelligence" is not something we are taught in school. In this case, it might be that your role is to help the person in question to access the support they need from somebody who does have the skills.

But in the instances where you do feel in a position to support a colleague further, a great first question to ask is "What do you think you should do?" or, alternatively, "What has worked for you in the past?" These simple lines of enquiry can go a long way to empowering the person to find their own answers. When people do this, it makes them feel more in control and therefore more secure.

Equipping the people in your workforce with the skills to effectively and holistically be available to one another during challenging times is a great step toward fostering connection, and in turn combatting the loneliness epidemic, at your workplace. When we delve a little bit deeper, becoming more curious, we see the "I" in front of us a little bit more clearly, and this can make all the difference to overall workplace well-being.

## ❋ Workbook

1. In the midst of difficulty, how comfortable do you feel with sitting in the "messy middle"? Are you in a rush to find a solution? Think about a time when someone came

to you with a concern. Did you allow the person the time to explore how they were feeling, or did you jump into the action phase? Journal about this experience and also about what you might have done differently. What questions could you ask in the future?

2. Is debriefing something you feel your workplace does well? When this is the case, it fosters understanding and creates a culture of care and concern. If your goal is a psychologically safe workplace, then this is an essential component. There might be someone in your organization who has skills in this area, or perhaps there is an organization you work with that can support your teams in developing this skill set. What do you think your first step might be? Who can you talk to or meet with to start exploring this a little further?

## "YOU" ARE JUST LIKE "ME"

I recently attended the funeral of my uncle and found myself part of a church service—not something that's part of my everyday life today but, as it is for many people, was something I took part in growing up. As part of the service, we took the time to wish one another well as we turned to those around us and said, "Peace be with you." This really struck a chord with me, and I enjoyed these moments of connecting, looking someone in the eye, and wishing them the best. The overall message for me was: "I see you, and I wish the best for you."

Church communities are experiencing dwindling numbers for many reasons, but one place we do still convene regularly with others is the workplace. Could it be that these spaces could benefit from some sort of practice like this?

I'm not suggesting bringing religion into the workplace, but, prior to dismissing the idea as far too fluffy, just think about how good it feels when someone acknowledges you in a genuine way. Instead, when somebody asks, "How are you?" the typical response is "Busy." When do people ever stop and say, "Well, you know, I had a pretty rough day yesterday, but I got a night's sleep last night and I'm feeling much better today. Thank you for asking." When somebody takes the time to see you, you feel better—and when we *feel* better, we *do* better. Isn't that what we want for the people on our team and for everybody who is part of our organization? The question then becomes which exercises or ways of incorporating these principles into your workplace will sit well with your work culture.

I have used a well-known spiritual practice called the "just like me" meditation with my own team and with plenty of other teams I've worked with. It might be something that you use at the beginning or the end of a meeting. For those not familiar with this practice, I have outlined a version below. To begin, you might ask people to close or lower their eyes, if this is something they're comfortable with. From there, ask the group to take a moment to consider the following:

- These people have feelings, emotions, and thoughts, just like me.
- These people have experienced physical and emotional pain and suffering, just like me.
- These people have at some point been sad, disappointed, angry, or hurt, just like me.
- These people have felt unworthy or inadequate, just like me.
- These people have worries and are frightened sometimes, just like me.

- These people wish to be happy, just like me.
- These people wish to be loved, just like me.
- These people have longed for friendship, just like me.
- Now, allow wishes for well-being to arise:
- I wish these people to have the strength, resources, and social support they need to navigate the difficulties in life with ease.
- I wish these people to be free from pain and suffering.
- I wish these people to be peaceful and happy.
- I wish these people to be loved . . . because these people are fellow human beings, just like me.[4]

Every single time I've used this exercise, it has generated some interesting discussion and sometimes even tears. In today's world, it can feel like we're living in a silo. But humans are pack animals, and history teaches us that we can only overcome adversity and achieve our goals together. This type of exercise reminds us that in so many ways, our life experiences, both good and bad, are shared, which in turn can bring us back to the understanding that we are part of something bigger.

I have also used "loving-kindness" practices in workplaces, where you extend kindness toward others and then yourself. You can start the exercise by asking those present to think of someone they are fond of and then send that person the following wishes:

- May you be happy.
- May you be healthy.
- May you have a peaceful mind.

Then ask the group to extend those wishes to someone in their broader circle, who perhaps they don't know as well:

- May they be happy.
- May they be healthy.
- May they have a peaceful mind.

Then, if people feel comfortable with this, you can ask them to extend the practice further to someone they find difficult to deal with (this can sometimes be a stretch, so you might also let people know they can pick another person from their broader circle):

- May they be happy.
- May they be healthy.
- May they have a peaceful mind.

Lastly, and most importantly, ask the group to extend those kind thoughts to themselves (this can be the hardest of all for those that like to give):

- May I be happy.
- May I be healthy.
- May I have a peaceful mind.

Alternatively, a lovely exercise that Priya Parker shares in her book, *The Art of Gathering*, involves going around the group from one person to the next and saying, "I see you, [insert name]," and that person responds, "I am here, [insert name]."[5] This might sound small, but I have found it to be really powerful in promoting that connection that we know will help our teams.

Realizing we are more alike than we are different, extending kind thoughts to others, or simply acknowledging that we are in this together can be a potent counterpoint to the us-versus-them mentality that often springs up in competitive corporate environments. Again, sometimes when we introduce these types of more spiritual exercises, they can feel a bit awkward or clunky, but I encourage you to give them a go. It's been interesting to witness the changes that occur when a workplace commits to this kind of practice. Some changes I have noted have been an overall greater tolerance for others and of the quirks we come with, becoming more aware of the people around you and attuned to some of the things they might be struggling with, and even small acts of kindness that perhaps make everyone's or one person's day a little brighter, and sometimes these things make all the difference.

It reminds me of something my mother once said to me after my father died. She said that she and my dad had led a relatively simple life. She said there weren't lots of big things but that Dad knew that she loved fresh lettuce, so he always made sure there was some in the garden for her, and this small thing made all the difference. Let's make sure that we don't underestimate the impact of the small things.

## ✳ *Workbook*

1. Here is a journaling prompt for you: How easily do you think the exercises above would fit into your workplace? Take some time to actually imagine your team participating, and if what comes up is a strong "hell no," consider why this is the case. Do you feel there's a resistance to seeing your colleagues as human beings? Has your workplace turned you into a team of robots?

2. Introducing some of these exercises at work might feel like a big leap. If this is the case, trial some of these practices at home or among friends at first. Once you've gotten comfortable with them, or even made them part of your own routine, you will feel more confident with

using them as a tool for connection. Which do you feel most drawn to? Personally I use the "loving-kindness" practice intermittently during the day. I find it helps me to remember the people I'm engaged with and not just get absorbed by the task at hand. It also reminds me to be kind to myself. What could you commit to?

## "COOKIE CUTTER" OR INNOVATION? IT'S UP TO "I"

This section poses a question for managers to ask themselves. Do you encourage people to be themselves? Do you mean it when you tell your team members to "be themselves," or do you secretly want them to be a little team of corporate clones? Having a team of clones is fine if you want a cookie-cutter approach to your business, every day just more of the same. However, if you want to encourage innovation and creativity (which, let's face it, we need more than ever to navigate the post-pandemic world), then you are only going to thrive when "be yourself" is part of the company DNA.

For example, do you know the individual "superpowers" of each of your team members? We certainly do not want to hide these. By celebrating who people are in their own unique way, you are taking a step forward in helping people to express their natural (and sometimes surprising) talents.

For example, it might be an artistic bent, a skill for fine detail, being great at organizing things and bringing events together, being fluent in a foreign language, or having a particular hobby. The list is endless, and I am sure you will be surprised just what comes up. I mentioned earlier that one of my team members has a penchant for poetry. I've also seen a team rally in a new way after a person's hidden talent for graphic design was uncovered (although you'd never have known it in the person's current role), and ever since, the artistic individual in question has been able to help their colleagues out with the design aspects of a presentation or create graphics for a company social media account. Another employee had majored in editing at university, and she discovered she was able to support the tenders and grants team to cast a very close eye over applications before they were submitted. We may also have yoga instructors in our midst, who can lead us during lunchtime sessions. Another company I work with had a team member (a lawyer by trade) whose superpower was singing; this was not something he used in the office, but once people found out, they enjoyed going to support him in his theater performances as a way to foster camaraderie on the team. Can you see the added benefit of getting to know one another a little better? You can't thrive trying to be someone else, but you can thrive at being more *you*—which I truly believe is the only way for people to flourish at work.

And we want our teams to be great, don't we? Or will "good enough" suffice? What we do know is that the world is changing faster than it ever has before. To respond and to meet this change with creative solutions, we are going to need sharp problem-solvers, innovators, and creators. The cookie-cutter approach is not going to work in the world that is already light-years ahead of us all. By encouraging our team members to truly be themselves and, in doing so, recognizing and celebrating the individuals on our teams and the unique characteristics they bring, perhaps we can all thrive. Personally, I believe this will bring us one step closer to being great.

## ✳ *Workbook*

---

1. Can you name the "superpowers" of each of your team-mates? As a team activity, ask people to bring along a list of what they see as their five superpowers to discuss with the group. I often do this exercise individually with people, and at the beginning people can feel really stumped trying to come up with their answers. If people get stuck, ask them to reflect on something they are proud of in their lives—maybe a big project that went well or a big team success—and from there drill down into what they contributed to this. Once people are able to see what their piece of the puzzle was, they will see that that is their superpower!

---

### MANAGERS: EVERYTHING TO EVERYONE? MAYBE NOT.

As supervisors, many of us try to be everything to everyone. But is this a realistic expectation? We each arrive at a workplace culture with such different backgrounds, having taken many different paths. Being relatable and available is certainly a strength for any manager, but can we be generous enough when we look at our teams to realize that there may be others who are more suited to developing skills for the different people on our teams? If we really are invested in people being themselves, embracing their "I" and not just behaving like corporate clones, then we need to understand that any one individual will not be able to provide them with everything they need. We will need to look more broadly at who else could support them in developing their particular skill set.

Think of this search as scrolling the internal "LinkedIn" of your organization, the better to support each individual being the best they can. This may or may not be down to the person's direct line manager. When I'm working with people, I often ask, "Who could you talk to about a concern?" People easily nominate someone who has experience in the area they want to work on, but 99 percent of the time they have not reached out for a coffee or tried to connect. So what stops us from reaching out and making connections outside of our immediate team at work? And, on a broader scale, how does your workplace encourage connection and generosity when people are developing their individual skills and career paths? Is it recognized that reaching further than your immediate team is beneficial, or is the expectation that your professional development will derive exclusively from your direct line manager?

In my opinion, we become our best "I" by learning from and being influenced by a number of different working styles. By expecting our team members to adhere to only one way of doing things, I believe we are holding them back. Certainly, my preferred working style—how I bring my "I" to the table—has been influenced by around five different people that have been mentors to me over the years. In combining all of their wisdom and applying it to my unique skill set, I am not a cookie cutter of Marg or Di or Suzanne or Judy; I am myself. If we are serious about allowing people to bring their "I" to work, it is important they are exposed to many different approaches to getting the job done. Does your workplace support the generosity that allows employees to learn from different people in your organization, so that they can be the best they can be?

## ✳ *Workbook*

1. If you are a manager, write down the names of the people on your team and what skills you think it would be best for them to work on next. Once you've done this, have

a good look at your list and think who the best people might be to support the development of those skills. You will obviously put your own name against some of these items, but there might be some areas that are not your strong suit. How can you support your team members' development by making sure they have access to different people and different points of view? How could being exposed to different working styles put them in a better position to develop a working style that they can call their own?

2. For those who are not managers, the question of course is who else could you be connecting with and learning from? Have a good think about the areas you want to work on in terms of your professional development and consider the people in your network who you could ask to mentor you. They might say "no" or "not now," but often people are flattered to be asked, and it ends up being a win for both parties.

---

Why is it so important to see the person who comes through the door at work? To recognize and welcome the "I"? We can go back to Archbishop Tutu's quote about needing to prevent people from falling into the river rather than just pulling them out. As someone who has worked with organizations for over twenty years, I can tell you it is much easier to prevent them from falling in; you just need to make it a priority. We get so caught up in our busy lives that we only stop and take notice when people are in trouble. Wouldn't it be refreshing to put in the resources early so they don't get into trouble in the first place? The "I" of the MAGIC framework is fundamental to this. We know that we do better when we are connected, and we have explored the loneliness epidemic and the spiraling mental health crises that we have been living with. Investing in people will quite simply help them to stay well at your workplace, and that makes a whole lot of sense from both an individual perspective and a work perspective.

Often we get this but we don't know where to start, so in this chapter we have looked at practical strategies you could implement at work. It might be pushing against the "busyness" and getting to know one another. You might give people the tools to be available to one another during challenges at work so that they feel supported. Maybe it is recognizing their strengths and making sure that our egos don't get in the way of others achieving their goals and taking up opportunities. All of these activities help us to focus on the "I." These types of activities will help your team to initially flourish personally, but then you will get the roll-on effect and your business will reap the benefits.

# CHAPTER 7

# CURIOSITY

*Let your curiosity be greater than your fear.*[1]
**—PEMA CHÖDRÖN**

**C**uriosity is essential for any organization's success—especially in our current climate. Navigating our post-pandemic world, with all its implications and unknowns, doing things "the way we always have" is simply not an option. And while it might seem safer to stick to a well-worn path, we need to see embracing curiosity as an opportunity and not a threat.

Unfortunately, in any organization that has become stuck in its ways, curiosity—which I use to refer to anytime we look at something from a different point of view—can be seen as an almost mutinous response to company culture and systems. We then react accordingly: we become defensive and respond to curiosity as a threat. We have all seen it. We see people shut out or shut down. But do we ever really know it all, or is it perhaps more often the case that we think we are supposed to? From the perspective of workplace well-being, either one of these attitudes is a little dangerous, as when we view enquiry as a threat, we start pushing against it and, consequently, one another, rather than leaning toward one another and working collaboratively. The brave new world we find ourselves in requires all forces working together to find the new post-pandemic path.

Curiosity is invaluable when it comes to problem-solving. I think most of us recognize at some level that the first iteration of a solution that occurs to us may not hold all the answers. Curiosity helps us to tease out the nuances that will take our problem-solving from good to great!

Curiosity is also essential elsewhere in the workplace. For instance, let's consider workplace conflict. When I am called in for a mediation, I always meet with the parties involved in the conflict individually prior to us all getting in a room together. So often, the story they each tell me of how they arrived at the place they find themselves is so different from person to person, I can barely believe they are talking about the same set of circumstances. Each person has become so "locked in" to their own version of events, they have almost created their own individual realities. As such, a resolution seems highly unlikely.

Now let's see what happens when curiosity is brought to the table. I might ask, "How do you think John or Mary sees things?" Or, "If John or Mary were sitting here, what would they be telling me?" I find it astonishing that for the most part, people have not even considered (or perhaps wanted to consider) how the other person might see things, let alone how their views might change were they to put themselves in the other person's shoes.

The fact that so much conflict comes back down to this attitude is an example of the trouble that can arise when an individual decides they "know it all." But too often, a corporate culture that rewards those who never show weakness or vulnerability, while punishing those who confess to not having all the answers, encourages this closed-minded, defensive thinking. Reversing this, and encouraging authenticity and space for people to not "know it all," provides the opportunity for a culture where people can ask questions to understand. Ultimately the solution from this scenario may very well be a better fit, as all the questions give you a broader understanding of the complexities of the issue at hand. This means looking closely not just at individual attitudes to curiosity but at the company culture as a whole.

Remember how one of the requirements for a healthy workplace is psychological safety? The goal of Google's Project Aristotle research was to discover the secrets to an effective team environment, and they defined psychological safety as a state where "teammates feel safe to take risks around their team members. They feel confident that no one on the team will embarrass or punish anyone else for admitting a mistake, asking a question, or offering a new idea."[2]

Curiosity is key to this, and in many ways the previous chapters have been paving the way for this work. If you've been engaging with the workbook exercises throughout, you will already have some practices in place for questioning how you do things in your workplace. People will have been encouraged to speak plainly in an authentic way and not be gobbled up by corporate speak; you will have ground rules in place so that everyone has a voice; and, by encouraging people to bring their "I" to work, you will be getting used to welcoming differing opinions and points of view.

In summary, the other pillars of this framework really help to build a curious workforce—but it's when we lean fully into curiosity, and really make it a part of our day-to-day, that the true magic can happen.

## CALM DOWN, DEAR

As mentioned, curiosity is especially helpful when it comes to conflict resolution. When someone has a different opinion from us, it can feel frustrating that they are unwilling to see things from our perspective. It can even seem as if they are challenging or attacking us. When this is the case, it can trigger a stress response, as if we were being physically set upon. With the adrenaline flowing, we then react (rather than respond) from our amygdala, the most primal and emotional part of our brain. Needless to say, this does not necessarily support positive team relationships. In fact, this kind of reactivity and "my way or the highway" mentality is at the core of most workplace conflicts.

Here are two ways in which this might play out. When our colleague offers a differing opinion, we can:

1. feel attacked, let the adrenaline rush, react, and attack back, or
2. take a moment and recognize our colleague simply has a differing opinion and that sometimes *we* find this challenging. From this place of awareness, we can allow the adrenaline to subside, take charge of our emotions, and get curious about the best way to respond to the situation presenting itself to us.

Option two often requires developing a mental "toolbox" to dip into when we feel challenged at work or as if we've been put on the spot—not the easiest once the adrenaline is in charge. The first tool, therefore, is awareness; we need to be able to identify when our logical mind is no longer running the show.

So, do you know when your stress response has been triggered? What does it feel like for you?

For me, the telltale sign is that my heart will start to race, or I will get an uncomfortable, heavy knot in my stomach. One of my clients said he literally feels the temperature rise in his body, while another said that the tone in her voice changes pitch. When she notices this shift, she knows she is in "reaction mode." Once you've noted that you are in reaction mode, you can ask yourself: *Do I need this shot of adrenaline to help me handle this situation?*

The answer might be yes if you realize you need to react quickly to an acute situation. Adrenaline is not always bad, and sometimes it is what we need to allow us to work through a challenge. We just need to ensure that it is a conscious process. Or the answer might be no if what's required is a more measured and considerate response. This is when to put in place strategies that we know will help us to step out of the adrenaline fugue, reset, and come back to the situation from a place that is more centered and calm.

Two of the reset strategies I teach are:

- Take a big breath into the belly. This activates the parasympathetic nervous system and helps to bring us out of the reactive state.
- Come back into the body. Feel your feet on the floor, your bottom in the chair, your hands on the table. This brings us out of fight-or-flight mode and back into the present moment.

And guess what: curiosity is another reset strategy. So often when we react disproportionately to a challenge to our way of doing things, it's because we are imagining all the things that could go wrong if we veer "off course." Based on past "failures," we leap to a worst-case scenario, envisioning a future that is not actually real. If instead we are able to observe the situation and get curious about all the possibilities that lie ahead, we may not feel quite so threatened, helping us to reset and get back to a place where we can respond.

In these situations, I often ask a question such as, "I had not thought of it from that perspective; how do you think that would work?" This immediately activates the prefrontal cortex, the part of our brain that is responsible for logical problem-solving. By bringing this part of our brain online, we can come out of that amygdala "hijack" and back into a space of creativity, cooperation, and collaboration. Not only does it create unnecessary stress for us as individuals when we react too quickly at work, but it can also have a huge impact on how we operate as a team. Instead of working together to find optimal solutions, we end up attacking one another and creating a climate of "blame and shame."

On the flip side, encouraging curiosity as a way to help people respond (rather than react) will foster a culture of innovation, debate, and healthy conflict resolution. By seeking to understand where another person is coming from, while managing our own emotions so as not to become defensive, we also have a better chance of exploring issues respectfully. Let's not forget, the pearl needs the grit—which means I'm not saying we can't disagree and thrash things out. Rather, coming from a place of curiosity means coming to these challenging conversations in a way that keeps everybody safe.

As a first step, simply knowing when you are feeling triggered will help you take a step back to consider what the best response might be, and in doing so you will reap the rewards. Not only will you avoid spinning off into a stress spiral; your teammates won't find themselves on the receiving end of an explosive outburst—something we have all born painful witness to at some point. This approach says to everybody on the team: *I see you, you are important, your opinion matters, and you need not fear retribution.*

Can you already see how this will start to create a space for MAGIC to happen?

## ❋ *Workbook*

1. Freewrite on the following journal prompt: What is your "tell"? How do you know you are in a space where you will react before you respond?

2. When you recognize this, what can you do to reset? I have listed some ideas above, but there are many ways to recenter ourselves when the amygdala has been hijacked. One of my clients notices things around the room to bring her into the present: the water jug, the clock. This helps to bring her out of her "monkey mind." Another client sips her water but takes time to notice the coolness of the glass and the taste of the water. What could you do to give yourself the space you need to hit the reset button?

3. What question can you have in your back pocket to use curiosity to reset? For example, it might be, "Can you tell me more about that idea?" or "Gee, that's a different way of looking at things. Can you give me a bit more detail?" Come up with three or four that feel like they "fit" you, and write them on a Post-it Note somewhere.

## A NEW PERSPECTIVE: MAKING SPACE FOR INNOVATION

We know that our brains crave certainty. We like to be able to see how things fit together and to have an answer at the ready. It makes us feel comfortable and in control, and we feel we can relax a little when everything is in order.

When we commit to curiosity, however, we may need to let go of some certainty and control, and this can make us feel *un*comfortable. As David Rock, cofounder and chief executive officer of NeuroLeadership Institute, describes, a sense of uncertainty about the future generates a strong threat or "alert"' response in your limbic system. Your brain detects something is wrong, and your ability to focus on other issues diminishes. Your brain doesn't like uncertainty—it's like a type of pain, something to be avoided.[3] So by exploring the best possible solution—not always the most obvious or convenient one—we often need to at least test out a number of ways of approaching something, not to mention, dare I say it, get a few things wrong before we get them right. This uncertainty can resemble "pain" and can make us feel like we have lost our way, but by consciously making an effort to try new things, we invariably pick up new insights that serve us in the long run.

Are you willing to sit with this discomfort in the name of innovation, or would you prefer to stick with the way things are and risk stagnating? Sometimes we like to wrap things up as quickly as possible, even when we know we'll only get a mediocre result. But if we're willing to follow our curiosity and tease things out a little more, we might end up somewhere really great.

So how do you actively promote this attitude in your workplace, without creating chaos? As we looked at earlier, solid ground rules can allow us to venture out and gain the opinions but still provide that tethering to bring us back to the task at hand and ensure an outcome is achieved. A positive first step—which we have explored elsewhere—is to encourage everyone to give their opinion about the way things should be done. Ensure people know you are interested in what they think by doing the following:

- Encourage activities where you get the group to brainstorm solutions. Getting everybody's ideas up on the board can really support curiosity and help you to explore all the options that might be available.
- Go around the group during meetings and give each person the chance to provide feedback on a current project. This is another way to ensure it is not just the same old (loudest) voices that get heard.
- Let your team know that you're always interested in hearing how they think things can be done more efficiently and more effectively and not just in keeping things as they are.

Once people get more practice using their voices in these situations, and, even more importantly, once they know it is safe to do so, then they will be more likely to continue to offer their ideas—one of which might be just the thing that gives your business a leading edge. The workplaces where employees get shot down for thinking differently or coming up with their own ideas are only holding themselves back.

During your recruitment process, you might ask people what innovations they've been involved with that they are proud of, which also signals to people that you are interested in hearing what they think about how things can be done. By including this in your recruitment process, you're seeding the idea that you like doing things a little differently right from square one.

## ✳ *Workbook*

1. For a team activity, think of a challenge your workplace is currently facing. This might be something external in your industry, it might involve your customers, or it might be an internal challenge you are facing or a process that

everyone knows is not working. Go around the group and get everyone to provide ideas about what changes could be made. Write everything that comes up on a whiteboard. Once you have gone around the group, get everyone to vote on the three ideas that they feel will make the most change, and then tally up these votes to come up with three you can start to work with. (And don't forget to keep a record of all the other ideas; if the first three are not successful, you have a plan B.)

2.  Delve into your own curiosity through freewriting on this journal prompt: What area of your working life currently isn't working, and how would you like it to change? Over a week, set aside ten minutes per day (I like to put a timer on) to write about what changes you could make in this area, and then put your writing away until the next day. At the end of the week, read through everything you have written. By spending a little longer with this prompt than usual, you might be surprised at what you come up with.

## CURIOUS CONVERSATIONS

Let's speak plainly here: Nothing is achieved by avoiding difficult conversations. Nothing! If we want to connect in a meaningful way, we need to be authentic with one another, and that means we are going to need to have discussions when we disagree. It also means providing feedback that people may not have been expecting or are not happy about.

I like the way that Jeff Weiner, who was once the CEO of LinkedIn, reframes these tough conversations in his discussions about compassionate leadership. He emphasizes that it is important to "work to understand how the other person's thinking is similar or different than your own, along with the reasons for this. Focus on learning from the other person's perspective. Then, use those learnings to improve your understanding of others and their situations, deepen your relationships, and broaden your overall thinking."[4] He also describes the importance of avoiding what I call the "head in the sand" approach that is so common—where everyone knows there's a problem but nobody talks about it (or at least not directly to the person involved). He reminds us that when we talk *to* the person, not *about* them, we are not only showing them respect but are also giving them the opportunity to course correct and make changes that might not only make a difference to our business but that also foster connection and psychological safety. Surely, we want this for the people we work alongside. If you want your people, your team, and your organization to be great, it requires tough conversations at times—and curiosity can help.

How? Because we are often nervous about these conversations in the first place, we tend to rush in without taking time to consider what might help our message land better. And I don't just mean book ending these discussions with "positives"—saying something "good" and *then* delivering the difficult news. People can smell this tactic a mile off and are usually just waiting for the bad news in this scenario. Instead, using curiosity when preparing for these conversations can help you workshop ways to use them to support your colleagues. For example:

- Write down everything you think the person does really well before you talk to them. It's important to keep the whole person in mind, as sometimes when approaching these types of conversations we can adopt a tunnel-visioned approach, focusing only on the problem. Simply keeping all their positive attributes in mind sets us up for a good result.

- Journal for ten minutes to provide some clarity around what you want to discuss. In this exercise, you might like to imagine some of the points the other person might raise and prepare a little for these as well. Sometimes we go into these scenarios without any curiosity about how the other person might be perceiving the situation.

- Bring your curiosity to the conversation itself, and make sure that you prepare questions in advance to really try to understand from the other person's viewpoint. This will take time, so make sure you have allocated enough time for the conversation to ask these questions and actually listen and try to understand the person's answers.

- Consider whether there is a way to compromise. I am always amazed at how many people come into a mediation thinking that they must get everything they want. When I ask them where the compromise is, they often express shock—and even indignation—but with a little curiosity, they can usually identify a few areas where they're open to some give-and-take. Reflect a little on what you actually need from the conversation and where you're prepared to compromise. This may seem tough at first, but all it requires is for you to be a little more curious.

## ✳ Workbook

1. Can you think of a difficult conversation from your past that went pear-shaped? Is there anything you recognize that you could have done differently that might have changed the outcome? Journal on what comes up.
2. Write down your own individual action plan for difficult conversations. Now that I've invited you to approach

them a little differently, what will you be mindful of before heading into a conversation where you need to deliver a difficult message? My favorite is considering the whole person, as this helps ensure I see beyond what isn't going right.

## FEED IT WITH FACTS

Uncertainty about the future leads to anxiety; fear of the unknown is not uncommon. In our current working environment, with so much in flux, this uncertainty can feel pretty constant. Unacknowledged, anxiety can be very disruptive for both you and your workplace, as it can manifest in individuals as self-doubt, aggression, or poor performance.

Curiosity can help manage some of these feelings. Faced with any unknown, ask yourself, *Do I have all the facts?* If the answer is no, then what research can you engage with to get a better understanding of what is going on? Is there someone you can talk with to get a little more clarity? Often when I meet with people, they will discuss concerns that they feel anxious about. When we tease the scenario out, often there are big gaps in terms of the facts, while they have jumped ahead and made assumptions about how things will play out. Unfortunately we know, as psychologist Dr. Rick Hanson says, that we have a negativity bias, so when we jump ahead, we land in scenarios with negative outcomes.[5] Clearly this is not going to be helpful. Once we see this is the case, we can engage curiosity to get a better idea of what's really going on and make a plan going forward. I call this exercise "Feed It with Facts."

Having looked at the same situation with a bit of curiosity, people are inevitably calmer when they follow up with me. Sometimes, all it took was for them to ask their manager for a more detailed update on the situation at hand. For example, I worked with a person whose company was going through a major restructure. In her mind, she saw her herself being transferred to all sorts of places, none of which seemed particularly appealing, and she lost a lot of sleep during this period. Following our session, she made time to ask her manager for an update and mentioned where she thought she might be headed. She was pleasantly surprised that her manager appeared bemused and could not quite understand how she'd come to that conclusion. She told her, "Of course you won't be going there; your strength is in this area, so we are looking at keeping you in this role." When she asked a little more, she found that not only was the role exactly what she wanted but that she would also be working with people she'd worked with before and really liked and respected from a professional perspective. All that lost sleep was for nothing—she just had to feed her anxiety with some facts!

In some instances, we can also tell ourselves that information is being purposely withheld from us, when in reality time is the culprit. Some of this again goes back to the negativity bias—we feel that something underhand must be going on. Whereas in reality people are often moving so quickly that they do not take the time to explain changes properly or to provide regular updates. However, when asked, our leaders are usually more than happy to let us know more about what's going on, and we realize there is nothing sinister going on after all. In the grips of workplace anxiety, ask yourself:

- Do I have enough facts? What information do I actually need to help me to feel more settled?
- How can communication channels be improved overall, to ensure that people are being kept in the loop?

Encouraging a culture of curiosity, where people feel free to ask questions about every aspect of the projects at hand, is a vital part of ensuring your team feels safe and secure. This means your team needs to know there is no such thing as a silly question and that they can reach out anytime they are feeling uncertain. Maybe "Feed It with Facts" can be one of your ground rules. This means arming people with as much intel as possible at each stage of a process, before anybody hits the "stress button" or starts cranking the office rumor mill. Various practices can be built into our day-to-day so that this becomes the norm.

A good place to start is to consider your communication channels, particularly during times of change when people may be working from home or switching to a different schedule. Do you always communicate transparently? Do you tell people as much as you can or as little as you need to? Sometimes it can feel like we're doing the right thing in protecting people from difficult news or that we're simplifying a process by glossing over complex details, and, yes, there is always a call to make. However, in my experience, the more people know about what's actually going on, the better.

In fact, I often encourage the organizations I work with to overcommunicate—especially during times of change or uncertainty. This means ensuring you are providing regular updates and using multiple different channels to relay your message. For example, this could mean speaking to your team as a group, speaking to individuals, and then following up via email—variety is important, as we all take in information differently. Most importantly, though, always end by asking, "Are there any questions?" It's important that you come to this last part from a genuine place and not just because you are ticking a box. This means keeping an open mind, engaging properly with anything that comes up, and making sure you have provided ample time for these questions to be answered. After all, something that may not be a big deal for you could be keeping somebody else awake at night. Giving them space to clear this up could be the difference between a coworker who is enthusiastically getting on with the job in hand and one who's ready to quit.

Of course, the honest answer to somebody's question might be "I don't know the answer to that, but I will certainly let you know when I do." Remember that we are also working on authentic conversation, and being real with others means it's also more than okay not to have all the answers.

The fact is, no matter how many facts we arm ourselves with, there will always be plenty of unknowns in our life. Some situations just aren't black-and-white, and facts are hard to find when we're wading through the gray. During periods of greater uncertainty, such as we have been faced with during the pandemic and which we will continue to be confronted with when it comes to climate change, we need to look instead to the routines and relationships that we can depend on to support us when nothing else feels certain. Staying curious can help here too; acknowledge that you have a lot of uncertainty at present, a lot of things you can't control. Remind yourself that our brains like certainty, so this lack of control makes you feel uncomfortable. Then ask yourself what are the routines you can build into your life or what relationships you can put more energy into to help you stay grounded. This will allow you to take back some control of your environment, and you might just find it eases some of those anxious feelings. Some new routines to get curious about might be:

- a cup of tea in the morning
- hosing the garden
- walking the dog
- setting new boundaries around email and social media
- regular exercise

- self-care by dressing up or not, whichever feels better for you
- mindfulness practices

Anything you know you can do regularly will help you to feel a little better. Once you have routines booked in, look toward the relationships that also help you to feel restored, and book those people in too! By setting up these routines and relationships, we become active participants in our own lives; it will no longer feel that life is just happening to us or around us, and this can help us to feel more comfortable.

## ✳ *Workbook*

1. The first step is to recognize when you are feeling anxious. Freewrite using this journal prompt: What are the signs that I am feeling anxiety?

2. When you notice these signs, what worst-case scenario is playing in your head, and how can you stop yourself from jumping ahead to what could happen? A client of mine has a big red stop sign on her desk that reminds her to regularly stop to consider if she is acting on what she knows or what she thinks might happen. How can you remind yourself not to jump ahead and to only respond when you know all the facts?

3. What practices does your workplace have in place that ensure people have the information they need to feel stable? Does your workplace have a "Feed It with Facts" mentality? If not, what might be the first step in implementing this?

## ARE WE CURIOUS WITH OURSELVES; ARE WE KIND?

Sometimes the people we are hardest on are ourselves, particularly when we're trying to live in a way that's aligned with our values. Feeling passionately about doing the right thing, and wanting to deliver on this and contribute something meaningful, can find us pushing ourselves to the limit. But if we push ourselves so hard that we fall over, we won't be any help to anyone.

Thankfully, the world is becoming a little savvier when it comes to the concept of self-care, and many of us are on board with having some good practices in place to help take care of ourselves. But one area we often still need to work on is the voice in our head with all the "shoulds" and "have tos." We are our own constant companions, which means it's important to be vigilant that you are treating yourself with respect. And curiosity can help in this area as well. It's not something many of us think about, but getting curious about how you talk to yourself can make a huge difference to overall levels of confidence and self-esteem—two other qualities we definitely want to be bringing to the workplace. Ask yourself: *Am I kind to myself, or am I more likely to berate, scold, and criticize myself because of all the things I "should" have done?*

Once you have started to monitor your own self-talk with curiosity, I will warn you, you might be shocked with what you hear. Think about how you could look at this differently or what you might say to a colleague or close friend in the same situation. You would probably say, "You are doing a great job."

# ✳ *Workbook*

1. Begin to pay attention to how you talk to yourself. Pick a day to listen in, and don't try to change the voice in your head; simply notice what it says and take some notes. Particularly notice the "shoulds" and "have tos."

2. On the following day, review your notes and consider where you could perhaps think of things from a different perspective. Pick one of your "shoulds"—"I should go to that meeting"; "I have to complete a certain task by 10:00 a.m."—and ask yourself if you do really need to go or whether that job needs to be done by 10:00 a.m. or if in fact it even needs to be done by you at all. I once had a client who could not leave her home until it looked a certain way; it was a big "should" for her that ultimately meant that she ended up running out of the house feeling somewhat frazzled before her workday even started. We explored the toll this "should" was taking on her and questioned whether she wanted to start her day feeling frazzled. The answer, of course, was no, and with this she became curious about what she could do to let go of this habit. As I mentioned, I am looking for a new perspective because sometimes we can really lock into rigid routines. While we know that ground rules are important to keep us steady, they can start to really strangle us if they do not offer any flexibility. If nothing else, hopefully the pandemic taught us that we can pivot, so how can you look at your life with curiosity? Where can you do things differently that might make your life a little easier, with not so much hustle and bustle and a little more flow?

3. Once we have gotten used to listening to our own self-talk, we can even use our curiosity to ask ourselves questions that will help us to broaden our outlook in other areas of

our lives. You might ask yourself, *How can I bring my best self to this project? What do I need today? How could I be a good friend or teammate? I have just finished a big project; what do I need to restore before I jump into the next one?* You might be surprised at how that voice in our head can actually be helpful.

---

I started writing about this MAGIC framework before the pandemic. Through over twenty years of working with organizations, I could see how curiosity presented opportunities for problem-solving and that when curiosity was not in the building, it resulted in a big barrier to team culture and cohesion. But what I use to think was merely important, I now think is vital for organizations and for people to thrive. I have seen in so many instances people and businesses trying to return to how things were without acknowledging that they will never be the same, but we need to find a new path in both our individual lives and our working lives. We also need to acknowledge the discomfort that comes with uncertainty and introduce strategies that will help us to manage during these challenging times. Even the awareness around our response to uncertainty and leaning toward this with curiosity can make a huge difference. Change is not going away. How can you embrace curiosity in your life?

# CHAPTER 8

# MAGIC IN ACTION

Most of us with an interest in workplace well-being have known for some time that the way we've been working has not been working. We've seen the threats to organizations and individuals alike looming. We've seen the mental health statistics spike. We have noticed people traipsing in and out of work, getting the job done but not feeling like they really "belong." We've also seen people almost taken hostage by their devices, with technology becoming the master calling all the shots. If you want to get a clear visual of the impact of the tech takeover of our world, then take a look at photographer Eric Pickersgill's *Removed* project. A series of portraits of people interacting with technology with the devices themselves photoshopped out of the images, the subjects look miserable and isolated, devoid of any signs of life.

Faced with the enormity of the mental health and loneliness statistics, it's easy to feel like we'll never be able to make a difference. And so we become paralyzed, reverting back to just making it through the day. But in the words of Antonio Machado, "a path is made by walking"[1]; sometimes we only need to be able to see the next step. And this is the real gift of MAGIC. Hopefully you are seeing the "next steps" for making work work again for you and your workplace already.

In the company I founded eighteen years ago, we have always been keen to understand the factors that really make work work. With each intervention we've conducted, we've put measures in place to understand the impact, resulting in some incredible statistics: Outcomes from the early intervention programs we've developed and implemented have seen 85 percent of people feeling they now had the tools to care for themselves at work; 94 percent indicated that they had more awareness of their own and others' mental health; and 88 percent stated they felt they had the ability to "bounce back" after difficult times. However, my personal favorite has been that 94 percent said they now felt they had the skills to provide support and assistance to their colleagues. As much as this work has been about improving workplace well-being, it is also about people connecting at work and looking after one another.

As successful as this work has been, for many, early intervention continues to be about looking for the signs—and for there to be "signs," people already need to be struggling. With this in mind, I became focused on going even further upstream to determine the factors that would stop people from even nearing the riverbank. As discussed, this is how I began to shape the framework that would become MAGIC. But I also realized it was time to view the potential impact of workplace well-being more broadly.

As you've engaged with the work in this book, I hope that you have been able to see the positive impact on your own approach to and engagement with the workplace. But how about we expand our thinking to include the possibility that the work we do can positively impact the overall health of both our teams and our wider community? This is where this work gets really exciting. I've seen with my own eyes the ripple effect on the wider population connected to workplaces where the health and well-being of employees is front and center, and I've shared some of these insights with you in these pages. I have seen firsthand, time and again, the positive impact of making work work again. It is so significant that we can no longer look away. In fact, I would argue that we need to focus on this issue as a priority.

Quite frankly, there has never been a better time to engage with this work. One upside of the pandemic is that it has put the issue of public health at the top of our agenda, and I think we should keep it there. This period of upheaval has shone an unforgiving light on all the cracks in the system, forcing us to look toward the human cost of the way we have been working. Moving forward, let's prioritize the mental and emotional well-being of our people as much as the physical, and let's commit to looking after one another in the process. Prioritizing our health at work is a vital piece of the community-wellness puzzle—because when people do well at work, they bring that healthy, happy person home, and everybody benefits. It really is as simple as that. What a tremendous foundation that allows families and communities in general to thrive.

In my profession, I am fortunate to be able to work with courageous organizations and individuals who are willing to do things differently and to chart a different path. Helping the person behind the job description feel valued and seen has been some of the most rewarding work of my career. When I started in this line of work over twenty-five years ago, occupational rehabilitation consultants were only called in when things were going really wrong and somebody had "fallen in the river." By the time an employee was off work and unable to cope, we were tasked with "fixing things." And while I enjoyed supporting people getting back to work, the importance of a person's professional occupation beyond being the means of their income was always clear to me. In the best-case scenarios, work brought them a sense of meaning and identity and was also a way of connecting with others. As the years passed, it became increasingly important for me to talk to workplaces about how to prevent people from falling in the river in the first place.

Fortunately, there were people in my orbit who were also ready to have that conversation. When it came to early intervention, we emphasized education, making sure people knew how to recognize the early warning signals that someone was not doing well. This meant people had to get off the "busy" train, focus less on the transactional nature of the job, and actually look at the person sitting next to them. This in turn led to the development of tools to help people regain their attention, so that they could approach their work with presence and intention. These are the tools I have introduced to you in these pages. The foundations of MAGIC, and the outcomes I have witnessed from having developed and implemented them over the last fifteen years, have given me hope that I am not alone in wanting something different.

After working in the early intervention space over such a long period, the precise elements that put the focus back on people and their humanity have become very clear to me. As discussed, it is out of this process that the MAGIC framework was developed. Having engaged with the work yourself, I am very interested to know what the impact has been for you. Have you noticed a difference with the way you connect with your work and your workplace? Which one of the pillars of MAGIC made the biggest difference for you? In my experience, most people find that one or two pieces in particular really resonate with them. Take a little time to reflect on what changes you have noticed. If some sections of the work didn't sit well with you, it is equally important to consider why that may be. It may be that nothing significant feels like it has shifted, and that's okay too. Sometimes we need to sit with these ideas for a little while to let them percolate, and you may find yourself coming back to the ideas and exercises in this book at a time further down the road.

Remember, this is not about a "quick fix." If anything, the role of MAGIC in the first instance is to provide you with an assessment tool to gauge how you are tracking—which is often the part that's missing. We have a sense that something is off, but rather than digging deeper into what this is and finding the root cause of the issue, we move straight into action. Common wisdom is that if there's a problem, we'd better get on it and fix it! But an approach whereby we plaster on a Band-Aid without really exploring where the gaps are and why is destined for disaster. Many of us have experienced well-intentioned workplace programs being implemented that felt more like they were about ticking a box than actually getting to the heart of the problem at hand. By taking the time to truly understand the impact of Meaning, Authenticity, Ground Rules, "I," and Curiosity, and by asking yourself as an individual and as an organization where you sit within each of these areas, you will begin to see where the cracks really are. Now, instead of a problem, you have a huge opportunity. Before action must come awareness, so if all you've got by the end of this book is a clearer idea of what's not working, you can congratulate yourself! You are so much better placed to see what's really needed going forward.

I have always been a fan of Leonard Cohen, and in fact I once spent a glorious week on the Greek island of Hydra, where he lived much of his later life. In his song "Anthem," he urges us to forget our "perfect" offerings because in everything, there is a crack—but that the crack is actually what allows the light to shine through.[2] So often when we see the crack, we either berate ourselves or get defensive, both of which lead to little positive change—and which are actually likely to find us getting even more stuck in a rut. It's when we can peer into the cracks with curiosity and see this process in and of itself as a means for positive change that we are really beginning to work MAGIC.

I also want to emphasize that bringing compassion to this process is fundamental to developing an action plan that supports us in achieving our goals moving forward. Too often, we take a robotic approach to problem-solving that emulates the very technologies and systems that may have led to our breakdown in the first place, without allowing ourselves or the people around us the luxury of being human. And while "luxury" might seem an unusual term to use here, I stand by it. Our humanity should be something we value highly and aspire to. But the quest for perfectionism has become so overwhelming that it is casting an extraordinary shadow on our ability to see ourselves as perfectly imperfect human beings first and foremost—and, in this, the potential to recognize what we need to thrive again.

Sitting with the discomfort of not always being right is the only way we learn. This in turn is how we equip ourselves to do things differently. It's also easy to get caught up in stories of blame and shame when we discover what's not working—but recognizing where we've gone off course, and choosing another path, is nothing to be ashamed of. It is the first step toward making work work again, and isn't that why we're here? So, as you continue to engage with the work in this book, and to consider how MAGIC might look for you, the first step is to get really honest about where things have gone wrong and why. Only then can you take the necessary steps to turn things around, and the framework outlined in these pages will help you in both phases.

And as challenging as the disruption to our workplaces caused by COVID-19 has been, I'll state again that the time is very much *now* to begin this work. I have seen a range of different responses to the pandemic. There are those keen to rush back to the office and pretend nothing ever happened, and there are those who would prefer to stay working from home forever. But both of these are a knee-jerk response. Our working world has been in a process of transformation for some time; COVID has simply sped things up. The real opportunity now—and finding real solutions to the threats to workplace well-being—requires a much more considered approach. Never has it been more appropriate to implement MAGIC—both as a means of addressing what sort of culture you want for your workplace going forward and for assessing our collective relationship to work within this new world order.

In closing, let's recap on the wider potential for change when we engage with this framework.

## MAKING MEANING

I spoke with a client this morning who has recently returned to a position she held over two years ago. Despite this seeming like a step down the ladder, she stated emphatically that she felt this was where she'd be able to make the most difference, and that the events of 2020 had made it really clear to her what was important and ultimately what she had to contribute. The position she had returned to may not have looked as good on her CV, but it provided her with meaning, something she knew she had to prioritize following the unprecedented events of the last few years.

This has been a common theme among clients and teams following the COVID "pause."

Across the board, people have been much more interested in exploring the meaning behind the work they do. I think this stems from the realization that work is an enormous part of our lives, and that given the investment of time and energy it requires of us, it must be approached mindfully and intentionally. We are all a little more aware of our mortality and the importance of how we spend our time, this finite resource we call life. For some, this has meant the meaning of our work has come into clearer focus; for others, it has changed what we find meaningful completely. And some have focused on finding meaning at work for the first time, as a way of anchoring in amid the storms we have found ourselves in.

## AUTHENTICALLY YOU

Without a doubt, everyone has a story from their experience of the pandemic, ranging from uncertainty about what the future held to heartbreaking grief and loss. With this in mind, it has never been more important to be available for one another in a real and authentic way. We need one another, and we need to hear one another's stories. But, sadly, with the news cycle and social media what it is, we have also reached a point where our concentration seems to be on the market to the highest (or, rather, the loudest) bidder. In order to be there for one another as we rebuild our lives, we need to reclaim the skills that allow us to focus on what's in front of us for any significant length of time, without our attention being diverted by the pull of technology or the hectic pace of life. This also means letting the person in front of us finish their sentence and get what they need to off their chest, without hijacking the conversation by going immediately into action mode or by deflecting or minimizing their experience because it's too uncomfortable for us to listen to.

Every time we make space for the whole person in front of us, we are choosing to honor both their authentic humanity and ours. And when we equip our workforce with these skills by providing the opportunity for our people to connect, we can combat the loneliness epidemic. At no time in history has the strength of the group, the team, or the tribe not been recognized as a means to achieving great things. Encouraging authenticity in the workplace will be the glue that helps our teams come together again.

## GOOD GROUND RULES

Throughout my working life, I have admired people's resilience and been inspired by what people can endure. But I have also seen people at their lowest points, and in many cases this is not brought about by what you'd expect. Remember the analogy of the seesaw? I use this to help people to understand that life events can sweep in at any time, causing us to lose our balance and fall over. Picturing the seesaw, you can almost feel the ups and downs of life and how destabilizing they can be—as well as how exhausting consistently trying to find your balance can be. The recent years have brought so many ups and downs that it can feel like we all need to regain our balance, and one way to do this is to pop some blocks under the ends of that seesaw to help us find our footing.

This is where ground rules come in, those practices and processes that we and our teams can come back to and rely on. This begins with deciding, together, how we are going to communicate, how we will make decisions, and how we will get stuff done in a way that also honors our humanity. From there, the specific ground rules that help stabilize your workplace and the people in it will be entirely unique to you. But finding and implementing them across every level of your business is an essential step in navigating the shifting terrain of our new work order.

## I AM HERE

We certainly all have a lot to do when it comes to charting a path forward! The year 2020 may have shone a light on what hasn't been working, but it posed more problems than it solved. In the wake of the pandemic, most of us feel that we are playing catch-up. But as we sprint toward some imaginary "new normal," I believe it is more important than ever to make room for everyone to have a say in what this looks like. This means making it feel safe for them to bring their "I" to work. As discussed, this does not happen automatically, and setting some clear ground rules in this area is a great place to start. When we allow people to have their voices, we empower them, in turn empowering the potential for our group.

Isn't that ultimately what we want for our workplaces, an environment where people feel they are bringing their best selves to the job? Simply put, this is not going to happen if they feel they need to "fit in" to be a part of your workplace. Rather, a person who is able to bring their whole self to work also brings focus and vigor and innovation because they are not distracted by trying to fit into some corporate mold. Yes, working this way requires more time, attention, listening, and nurturing. But ensuring that people are seen and heard for who they are is an investment that's always returned with interest. After all, we need ideas from unexpected places now more than ever.

## STAYING CURIOUS

You might think curiosity would become the norm as we navigate uncharted waters. But when faced with overwhelming change, most people's natural inclination is to want to go back to what they know. But the world has changed, and we need to be willing to change and evolve with the times to accommodate our new normal and move forward. The businesses that will thrive in a post-pandemic world are the ones that stay curious and that see this as fundamental to who they are and how they work.

In 2020, I saw teams "leap tall buildings" as they came to the challenges posed by COVID with beginners' eyes and simply asked questions like "How are we going to make this work?"; "How will our small business stay afloat?"; "How will we juggle work with homeschooling?"; "How can our teams stay connected?"; and "How can we help ensure that those experiencing homelessness are supported through the pandemic?" The solutions we found to all of the above were made possible because of curiosity, creativity, and innovation. I have a client who keeps a picture of Curious George on her desk as a reminder to stay curious. She tells me that as soon as she rushes to respond to an email with "no," she stands back and asks herself, *What do I need to know before I make this decision?* A picture of Curious George might not be for everybody, but how can you make curiosity part of your workplace DNA? The key is to seek first to understand and then to be understood.

As we part ways, I want to share a final personal story that really brings home the importance of looking toward our people first and foremost for me, as well as the health benefits of making work work. Earlier in this book, I told the story of my Grandmother Flo and how, after she lost her husband, a community-minded workplace supported her and helped her family to stay afloat. When his father died, my dad was a month away from his third birthday, and from that day on he developed a significant stutter. When Dad went on to leave school at age sixteen, the principal told my grandmother that my dad should probably find a job in a back room where he would not be seen or need to speak to people. This was the 1950s, and instead of recognizing that people who stutter are sometimes unable to produce certain sounds, this difficulty was seen as being somehow tied to a person's intellect. Instead of feeling downhearted at this, the conversation actually provided just the challenge Dad needed to take the first step. He hadn't mapped out where he was going, but he was determined to get a job that reflected what he felt he had to offer.

Not only did he go on to work in a busy governmental department; he also volunteered his time and worked with a number of charities. He knew that in both of these roles, he would need to speak to lots of people and even speak publicly. Meaning he intuitively knew the value of engaging with his occupation as a means of therapy to support him in learning to speak more fluently—which was his goal. He also knew that he needed to speak, as challenging as it was for him, if he was going to learn the strategies that would ultimately help him speak fluently—such as learning which sounds gave him particular difficulty. He would never have developed these strategies in a backroom job where he didn't speak to anyone. He used the way he occupied his time as his own speech therapy.

Certainly, by the time I was born, he had come a long way toward achieving his goals. He had also intuitively been engaging with the pillars of MAGIC. He volunteered for causes that were important to him in order to give his work meaning. He found workplaces that valued their people and could see the authentic man he was beyond his stutter. He developed strategies to support himself and his speech, his ground rules. He was also unapologetically himself; he experienced many episodes of humiliation as a result of people's reactions to his stutter—some that I witnessed later in his life and some that he told me about. But he consistently and courageously brought his "I" to work every day. Finally, of course, curiosity was the key to finding a solution that worked for him when nobody else would believe in him: engagement with occupation. So, long before I developed the MAGIC framework, this approach to work changed my dad's life—something that my brother and I have been the direct beneficiaries of.

With these stories in my family history, I have lived and breathed the benefits of workplace well-being and of people feeling supported in their whole humanity by their occupations. I know firsthand just how powerful this can be, for individuals, for their families, and for their wider communities. In my own working life, I have encountered endless stories of people just like my dad and his mother, whose lives were changed by the fact that their employers saw beyond their abilities to deliver products or services and into the people at the core of their businesses. Employers who understood that for their people, a person's place of work could have a significant impact in their broader lives and well-being.

Surely now is the time to make workplace well-being a priority in all of our lives. Faced with so many unknowns, why not use this as an opportunity to build something we can be proud of? My vision going forward is for a workforce where individuals and communities all thrive as a result of the work we do, and where the workplace once again becomes a place that contributes to the overall health and well-being of all who engage with it. I know there will always be business owners out there who may not feel that this is their responsibility, who are not ready, for whatever reason, to make this investment in their people. But I have seen, time and again, that by looking away from the human issues impacting the people that make up your organization, you are also ultimately looking away from the overall success of your business as a player in the wider world. And who knew that all it really takes to make this dream a reality, and to stop our people from falling in the river, is a little MAGIC?

# NOTES

---

## INTRODUCTION:

1. Evelyn Lau, "A Look Back at Desmond Tutu's Greatest Quotes, from Kindness to Forgiveness," *National* (UAE), December 26, 2021, https://www.thenationalnews.com /arts-culture/books/2021/12/26/a-look-back-at-desmond -tutus-greatest-quotes-from-kindness-to-forgiveness/.

2. Royal Australasian College of Physicians, *Australian Health Benefits of Good Work Signatory Steering Group: Making It Happen*, 2018, https://www.racp.edu.au/docs /default-source/policy-and-adv/afoem/hbgw/hbgw-signatory -steering-group-flyer-2018.pdf?sfvrsn=265b0d1a_4.

## CHAPTER 1:

1. William Craig, "The Importance of Creating Sustainable Employees in the Workplace," *Forbes*, June 19, 2018, https://www.forbes.com/sites/williamcraig/2018/06/19/the -importance-of-creating-sustainable-employees-in-the -workplace/?sh=20d2f40c7285.

2. Coleman A. Baker, Phd, (2018, January 24). "Between Stimulus and Response, There Is a Space," *Medium*, January 24, 2018, https://medium.com/@colemanabaker/between -stimulus-and-response-there-is-a-space-ad5261e3c74e.

3. Gordon Waddell and A. Kim Burton, *Is Work Good for Your Health and Well-Being?* (London: TSO, 2006), https:// cardinal-management.co.uk/wp-content/uploads/2016/04 /Burton-Waddell-is-work-good-for-you.pdf.

4. Valerie Bolden-Barrett, "Study: Turnover Costs Employers $15,000 per Worker," *HR Dive*, August 11, 2017, https:// www.hrdive.com/news/study-turnover-costs-employers -15000-per-worker/449142/.

5. Safe Work Australia, *Managing Psychosocial Hazards at Work: Code of Practice*, July 2022, https://www.safeworkaustralia. gov.au/sites/default/files/2022-07/model_code_of_practice_-_ managing_psychosocial_hazards_at_work.pdf.

6. Helen Hawkes, "Get Smart with Mental Health," *Intheblack: Mental Health and Wellbeing*, October 2020, https://intheblack.cpaaustralia.com.au/-/media/project/cpa /intheblack/documents/magazines/2020-10-intheblack -mental-health-and-wellbeing.pdf.

7. Michelle H. Lim, "Is Loneliness Australia's Next Public Health Epidemic?" *InPsych* 40, no. 4 (August 2018), https://psychology.org.au/for-members/publications /inpsych/2018/august-issue-4/is-loneliness-australia-next -public-health-epide.

8. Howard Meltzer, Paul Bebbington, Michael S. Dennis, Rachel Jenkins, Sally McManus, and Traolach S. Brugha,

"Feelings of Loneliness among Adults with Mental Disorder," *Social Psychiatry and Psychiatric Epidemiology* 48, no. 1 (January 2013): 5–13, https://doi.org/10.1007/s00127-012-0515-8.

9. Australian Psychological Society and Swinburne University, *Australian Loneliness Report*, November 2018, https://researchbank.swinburne.edu.au/file/c1d9cd16-ddbe-417f-bbc4-3d499e95bdec/1/2018-australian_loneliness_report.pdf.

10. John Murphy, "New Epidemic Affects Nearly Half of American Adults," *MDLinx*, January 10, 2019, https://www.mdlinx.com/article/new-epidemic-affects-nearly-half-of-american-adults/lfc-3272.

11. Johann Hari, *Lost Connections: Uncovering the Real Causes of Depression—and the Unexpected Solutions* (New York: Bloomsbury, 2018).

12. International Labour Organization, "More Than 60 Per Cent of the World's Employed Population Are in the Informal Economy" (press release), April 30, 2018, https://www.ilo.org/global/about-the-ilo/newsroom/news/WCMS_627189/lang--en/index.htm.

13. CBS Broadcasting, "Silicon Valley 'Brain Hacking' Makes Smartphones Addictive," April 10, 2017, https://www.cbsnews.com/sanfrancisco/news/60-minutes-silicon-valley-brain-hacking-smartphone-addiction/.

14. Aran Ali, "The Rise and Rise of Media on Your Mobile Phone—in One Chart," World Economic Forum, May 3, 2021, https://www.weforum.org/agenda/2021/05

/rise-of-media-on-mobile-phone-chart/#:~:text=In%20
fact%2C%20every%20category%20with.

## CHAPTER 2:

1. Antonio Machado, *There Is No Road* (Buffalo, NY: White Pine, 2003).

2. Chris Hanlon, "On Fake Emerson Quotes," *Avidly*, August 27, 2019, https://avidly.lareviewofbooks.org/2019/08/27/on-fake-emerson-quotes/.

3. Carol Black, *Working for a Healthier Tomorrow: Work and Health in Britain* (London: TSO, March 17, 2008), https://assets.publishing.service.gov.uk/government/uploads/system/uploads/attachment_data/file/209782/hwwb-working-for-a-healthier-tomorrow.pdf.

## CHAPTER 3:

1. WorkHuman Research Institute, *Bringing More Humanity to Recognition, Performance, and Life at Work*, 2017, https://www.workhuman.com/resources/reports-guides/bringing-more-humanity-to-recognition-performance-and-life-at-work.

2. Friedrich Wilhelm Nietzsche (1974). *Twilight of the idols: or, how to philosophise with the hammer; The Anti-Christ; Notes to Zarathustra and Eternal recurrence.* New York: Gordon Press.

3. Johann Hari, *Lost Connections: Uncovering the Real Causes of Depression—and the Unexpected Solutions* (New York: Bloomsbury, 2018).

4. Brené Brown, "The One Problem with Feeling Joyful (and How to Fix It)," *HuffPost*, November 27, 2013, https://www.huffpost.com/entry/finding-happiness-brene-brown_n_4312653.

**CHAPTER 4:**

1. Johann Hari, *Lost Connections: Uncovering the Real Causes of Depression—and the Unexpected Solutions* (New York: Bloomsbury, 2018).

2. *Oxford English Dictionary*, 2nd ed. (1989), s.v. "authentic."

3. Drake Baer, "One of America's Most Beloved Authors Just Told Us Her 'Number One Life Hack' for Lasting Relationships," *Tech Insider*, August 26, 2015, https://www.businessinsider.com/brene-browns-biggest-life-hack-is-a-simple-phrase-2015-8.

4. Portia Nelson, *There's a Hole in My Sidewalk: The Romance of Self-Discovery* (New York: Atria, 2012), xi–xii.

**CHAPTER 5:**

1. Rho Sandberg, "The Costs of Conflict," *AIM Education & Training* (blog), Australian Institute of Management, August 1, 2007, https://www.aim.com.au/blog/the-costs-of-conflict.

2. Steve Bradt, "Wandering Mind Not a Happy Mind," *Harvard Gazette*, November 11, 2020, https://news.harvard.edu/gazette/story/2010/11/wandering-mind-not-a-happy-mind/.

3. Martin E. P. Seligman, *Flourish: A Visionary New Understanding of Happiness and Well-Being* (New York: Free Press, 2011), 33.

**CHAPTER 6:**

1. "Maya Angelou: In Her Own Words," *BBC News*, May 28, 2014, https://www.bbc.com/news/world-us-canada-27610770.

2. Australian Psychological Society and Swinburne University, *Australian Loneliness Report*, November 2018, https://researchbank.swinburne.edu.au/file/c1d9cd16-ddbe-417f-bbc4-3d499e95bdec/1/2018-australian_loneliness_report.pdf.

3. International Labour Organization, "More Than 60 Per Cent of the World's Employed Population Are in the Informal Economy" (press release), April 30, 2018, https://www.ilo.org/global/about-the-ilo/newsroom/news/WCMS_627189/lang--en/index.htm.

4. Ram Dass and Mirabai Bush, "Just-Like-Me Compassion Meditation," Spirituality & Practice (website), accessed May 11, 2023, https://www.spiritualityandpractice.com/practices/practices/view/27782/just-like-me-compassion-meditation.

5. Priya Parker, *The Art of Gathering: How We Meet and Why It Matters* (New York: Riverhead Books, 2020).

**CHAPTER 7:**

1. Pema Chödrön, *The Wisdom of No Escape: And the Path of Loving-Kindness* (Boulder, CO: Shambhala, 2018).

2. Google, "Guide: Understand Team Effectiveness," re:Work (website), accessed May 11, 2023, https://rework. withgoogle.com/print/guides/5721312655835136/.

3. David Rock, *Your Brain at Work: Strategies for Overcoming Distraction, Regaining Focus, and Working Smarter All Day Long* (New York: HarperCollins, 2009).

4. Justin Bariso, "The Enormously Popular CEO of LinkedIn Shares the Leadership Advice He Says Could 'Change the Game,'" *Business Insider*, September 21, 2017, https://www .businessinsider.com/leadership-advice-from-linkedin-ceo -jeff-weiner-2017-9.

5. Rick Hanson, "Confronting the Negativity Bias," *Rick Hanson, Ph.D.* (blog), October 26, 2010, https://www.rick hanson.net/how-your-brain-makes-you-easily-intimidated/.

**CHAPTER 8:**

1. Antonio Machado, There Is No Road (Buffalo, NY: White Pine, 2003).

2. Richard Gehr, "Leonard Cohen: 20 Essential Songs," *Rolling Stone*, November 11, 2016, https://www.rolling stone.com/music/music-lists/leonard-cohen-20-essential -songs-114187/.

# ACKNOWLEDGMENTS

I wish to acknowledge the Turrbal people as the Traditional Custodians of Meanjin (Brisbane), the lands on which I wrote *Work Your Magic*. I pay respect to Turrbal Elders past and present.

In *Work Your Magic*, I reference the power of the sliding-door moments in your life, and certainly this book would not be here without a number of those sliding doors.

Firstly, I would like to thank the following people, without whose involvement I would never have started this project:

Judy McLennan, who funnily enough I ran into in a bookstore many years ago and who gently suggested I should look into working in occupational rehab as a career. I have loved my work (almost) every day since that meeting.

Lori Schwanbeck. I was fortunate enough to study with Lori and Marc Lesser in the Search Inside Yourself program. After the course finished, I continued to work with Lori, and she suggested I write an article on a mindfulness exercise that I was doing with a group at a workplace. Before that time, I never considered myself a writer. Thank you for opening that door, Lori.

A lovely client of mine—a client who shared with me her book ideas and, with that, planted a seed that a book might be something I could also think about.

I would also like to thank those people who supported me in getting the book from the idea phase to being published:

Ruby Warrington, who edited the book for me and was extraordinarily kind with this first-time author.

Brooke Warner, for taking on a first-time author (there were a number of noes before I got to this yes).

Shannon Green, for her patience. This publishing world was completely new, and I was never quite sure of the next step; thank you, Shannon, for keeping me on track.

Laura Marie Lombardi from Laura Marie PR and Julia Ferracane from Righteous PR. If I thought publishing was another world, PR was again a completely new world to me. Thank you for being excited about the book and for helping me to get it out into the world!

Writing and publishing can feel a little isolating, so I am extraordinarily grateful to have met Ellen Devries and for her support with my social media but to also feel I had a teammate to walk alongside. Your friendship has meant a lot to me; thank you!

There have been a number of people who have been very generous with their time as I navigated the road from writing to publishing to promoting this book. I would like to thank Tina Tower, Michelle Broadbent, Kate James, Colleen McCann, Barrett Briske, Krissa Lagos, Nadine Anderson, Helen Jacobs, Mariah Neaumaier, and Andrea Clarke.

I would like to thank the team at Strive Occupational Rehabilitation for testing out the book for me and for being excited with me at all the different milestones.

Thank you to all my friends who checked in and asked how the book was going; it has been a long road, so I appreciate you hanging in there with me. A special thank-you to Rachel, who turned up on my doorstep with a bottle of champagne the day I signed my publishing contract.

Of course, having read the book, you would realize there would be no book without the story of my grandmother Florence "Flo" Darmody. I have always been acutely aware as a woman how fortunate I have been to have come from a long line of strong women (from both sides of my family). *Work Your Magic* also outlines some of my dad's story; the way in which he led his life with such courage has always been an inspiration for me.

To end, I would like to thank my family. In these uncertain times, I feel fortunate to have such a strong home base and fantastic group of people in my corner.

To Trice, Carlton, Andrew, and Cameron: I'm looking forward to many more get-togethers, holidays, and Christmases. One of my happiest places is sitting at your kitchen bench with champagne in hand!

I would also like to remember my mother-in-law, Pat, who is no longer with us but who has been another great female role model for me in resilience and the capacity to keep getting back up during tough times!

I have always felt lucky to have Mary as my Mum; for those of you that know her, you will know why. Most of all, I love that she allows me to be myself. That is a tremendous gift for a mother to give her daughter, and I hope I can keep that front of mind with my children.

I only have one brother, so I feel that I won the lottery getting you, Michael, and that I perhaps won it again when you met Victor. I love traveling through life with you both!

To my cousin Kris: I always look forward to the next conversation where we pick up just where we left off even though, sometimes, it's been months; everyone needs that person in their lives. Here is to more adventures with you and Cath.

I think for most of us that are parents, we feel that our children are our best teachers; I have learned so much from my children and feel grateful every day for having you all in my life!

My stepson Sean as a photographer has shined light on creativity and the importance of committing to your projects and purpose. My stepdaughter Georgie has taught me tenacity; she proves that staying focused and committed to hard work helps you to achieve your goals. My daughter Claudia's keen curiosity has been an important factor in my ability to question and open my mind to what can be. In a world that feels like it is increasingly hard, my daughter Sasha's kindness gives me hope. I would also like to thank both Hilde and Matt for welcoming a stepmother-in-law so warmly! And, of course, our gorgeous little Reign, who arrived in 2021, for giving us all a reason to smile after a tough couple of years.

Lastly, thank you to my husband, Chris, my number one supporter. I look forward to many more dog walks with you, where we solve the problems of the world. I love you.

# ABOUT THE AUTHOR

**SHARON DARMODY** is an organizational coach and mediator and the founding director of Strive Occupational Rehabilitation, which she launched in 2004 with the aim of helping to support people to be more engaged at work so that they can thrive both at work and at home. Sharon graduated from the University of Queensland in 1992 with a bachelor's degree in occupational therapy. Since then, she has completed Workplace Mediator training with Bond University, The Cinergy Conflict Coaching Model from Canada, Acceptance and Commitment Therapy, and was one of only 70 in Australia to complete Google's Search Inside Yourself six-month training course, which incorporates organizational mindfulness, emotional intelligence, and leadership tools. A huge fan of good seafood, great books, and swimming and walking at the beach, Sharon lives in Brisbane, Australia.

*Author photo © Milina Opsenica*

# SELECTED TITLES FROM SHE WRITES PRESS

She Writes Press is an independent publishing company founded to serve women writers everywhere. Visit us at www.shewritespress.com.

*Drop In: Lead with Deeper Presence and Courage* by Sara Harvey Yao. $14.95, 978-1-63152-161-4. A compelling explanation about why being present is so challenging and how leaders can access clarity, connection, and courage in the midst of their chaotic lives, inside and outside of work.

*Happier At Work* by Gayle van Gils. $16.95, 978-1-63152-204-8. Practical applications of mindfulness and compassion, along with inspiring stories of companies who apply these principles, for the more than 70 percent of people in US workplaces who are disengaged and stressed.

*The Clarity Effect: How Being More Present Can Transform Your Work and Life* by Sarah Harvey Yao. $16.95, 978-1-63152-958-0. A practical, strategy-filled guide for stressed professionals looking for clarity, strength, and joy in their work and home lives.

*The Way of the Mysterial Woman: Upgrading How You Live, Love, and Lead* by Suzanne Anderson, MA and Susan Cannon, PhD. $24.95, 978-1-63152-081-5. A revolutionary yet practical road map for upgrading your life, work, and relationships that reveals how your choice to transform is part of an astonishing future trend.

*This Way Up: Seven Tools for Unleashing Your Creative Self and Transforming Your Life* by Patti Clark. $16.95, 978-1-63152-028-0. A story of healing for women who yearn to lead a fuller life, accompanied by a workbook designed to help readers work through personal challenges, discover new inspiration, and harness their creative power.

*People Leadership: 30 Proven Strategies to Ensure Your Team's Success* by Gina Folk. $24.95, 978-1-63152-915-3. Longtime manager Gina Folk provides thirty effective ways for any individual managing or supervising others to reignite their team and become a successful—and beloved—people leader.